THE SWASTIKA: *SYMBOL BEYOND REDEMPTION?*

THE SWASTIKA:
SYMBOL BEYOND REDEMPTION?

STEVEN HELLER • JEFF ROTH, researcher

ALLWORTH PRESS
NEW YORK

School of
VISUAL ARTS

20 19 18 17   05 04 03 02

Published by Allworth Press
An imprint of Allworth Communications
10 East 23rd Street, New York, NY 10010

Cover design by Mirko Ilic, New York, NY

Original interior concept by Mirko Ilic, New York, NY

Page composition/typography by Sharp Des!gns, Lansing, MI

LIBRARY OF CONGRESS CATALOG-IN-PUBLICATION DATA

Heller, Steven
   The Swastika: a symbol beyond redemption? / Steven Heller.
      p.   cm.
   Includes bibliographical references and index.
   ISBN-10: 1-58115-507-7 (paperback)
   ISBN-13: 978-1-58115-507-5 (paperback)
   1. Swastika—History. I. Title.

BL604.S8 H45 2000
302.2'223—dc21
99-087040

Contents

Acknowledgements

Originally this book was turned down by a number of publishers, so I decided to publish it myself. Two people dissuaded me: One, Mirko Ilic, who designed the cover and the original format, believed that a limited print run and even smaller distribution would not do justice to the subject and urged me to reconsider. He then worked closely on the preliminary aspects of the presentation. The other, Tad Crawford, publisher of Allworth Press, who has always been supportive, was excited by this project from the moment I approached him and threw his full support behind it. Thank you both.

The research required much time and effort uncovering long-lost documents and rare artifacts. Much gratitude goes to Jeff Roth, my chief researcher, without whom there would be no book. Thanks also to Vicki Gold Levi, who helped locate some of the many objects shown throughout. In addition, knowing of my obsession, the following friends have provided valuable materials for my use: Art Chantry, Seymour Chwast, Sue Coe, Dr. James Fraser, Sybille Fraser, Christoph Neimann, Steven Guarnaccia, Rick Poynor, J. J. Sedelmaier, Victor Margolin, Nina Subin, James Victore, Art Speigelman, and Mark Podwal.

A few of the essays herein originated in different forms in other publications. I want to thank these editors for their support and encouragement: Martin Fox of Print, Julie Lasky, formerly of *Print*, and Neil Feinman, formerly of *Speak*.

I am also indebted to Eliot Weinberger for his careful reading of this manuscript and important suggestions.

Finally, thanks to Nicole Potter, Jamie Kijowski, and Anne Hellman, editors, and Bob Porter, Associate Publisher, at Allworth Press for their continued efforts on behalf of this book, and to Charlie Sharp at Sharp Des!gns, who skillfully finessed the final page design.

chapter one

SYMBOL BEYOND REDEMPTION?

In a solemn ceremony, representatives of four Arizona Indian tribes, resentful at Nazi "sets of oppression," forswore use of the swastika design in native basket and blanket weaving. The Indians placed a blanket, a basket, and some hand-decorated clothing, all bearing swastikas, in a pile, sprinkled them with colored sand and set them afire.

—*The New York Times*, February 29, 1940

The swastika holds a special fascination for graphic designers, like myself, who work with trademarks and logos all the time. After all, it is one of the most visually powerful symbols ever devised. Just set aside for a moment what is known about it and compare the swastika to other great signs of the past and present: No other mark—not even variations of the cross or, for that matter, the Nike swoosh—are as graphically potent. Like most effective symbols, the swastika's geometric purity allows for legibility at any size and distance, and when on its axis, the whirling square gives the illusion of movement. Like a propeller, its hooked edges cut through any surface on which it appears. And because of this, when we return to the swastika's significance during the twentieth century, it also cuts right through the heart.

The swastika's sublime form wed to its wicked function has stimulated considerable inquiry into its origins and its future. "The fact that an ignominious fanatic placed a swastika on his battle flag is insufficient reason for ignoring this symbol's historic significance," wrote the industrial designer Henry Dreyfuss in *Symbol Sourcebook: An Authoritative Guide to International Graphic Symbols* (John Wiley & Sons, 1997). Indeed, much has been written about the swastika's rhetorical metamorphosis from a token of good fortune into the emblem of Nazi Germany—as well as its continued use by hate groups throughout the world. The very currency of the swastika makes it a subject for fierce debate.

Today, simply uttering the word "swastika" evokes revulsion, indeed terror, in many. Yet by all accounts, throughout most of its long history, the swastika, the Zelig of all symbols, was comparatively benign. Prior to its transfiguration, it served as religious phylactery, occult talisman, scientific symbol, guild emblem, meteorological implement, commercial trademark, architectural ornament, printing fleuron, and military insignia.

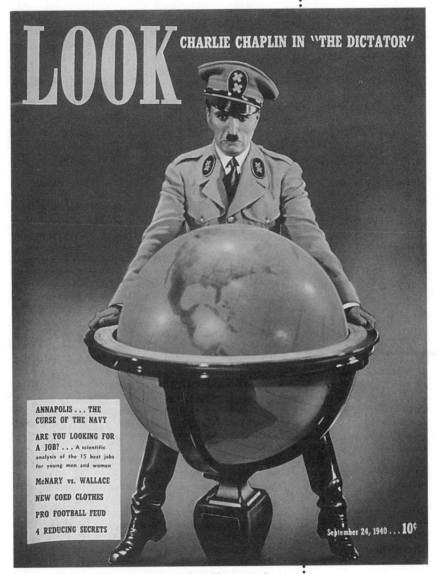

Look magazine cover. Charlie Chaplin as the Great Dictator wearing the sign of the "double cross," 1940.

"In the first instance probably the swastika may have represented the course of the sun in the heavens revolving normally from left to right," wrote H. J. D. Astley in "The Swastika: A Study" (*The Quest*, 1925). The swastika also symbolized light or the god of light, forked lightning, rain, and water. It is believed to be the oldest Aryan symbol and has been established as a Jain icon typifying animal, human, and celestial life. It represents Brahma, Vishnu, and Siva—Creator, Preserver, Destroyer. It appears in the footprints of Buddha, engraved upon the solid rock of the mountains of India. It stood for Jupiter Tonans and Pluvius of the Latins, and Thor of the Scandinavians. It is said to have had a relationship to the Lotus sign of Egypt and Persia. It appears on the Necropolis of Koban in the Caucasus. It has had a phallic meaning and has been recognized as representing the generative principle of mankind, making it the symbol of the female. Its appearance on monuments to the goddesses Artemis, Hera, Demeter, Astarte, and the Chaldean Nana gives it credence as a sign of fertility.

Its roots dig into deep regions of prehistory and emerge in antiquity. In 1874, Dr. Heinrich Schliemann discovered swastika decorations during his archeological excavation of Homer's Troy. He later traced similar

Swastika graffiti on building in postwar Germany, c. 1954.

iterations to, among other realms, Mycenae, Babylonia, Tibet, Greece, Ashanti on the Gold Coast of Africa, Gaza, Lapland, Paraguay, and Asia Minor. It was discovered painted or etched into Etruscan pottery, Cyprian vases, and Corinthian coins. Schliemann claimed that as described in Ezekiel 9:4, the swastika was similar to the ancient Hebrew letter tau, the sign of life, which was ritualistically written on the forehead of its believers (the reason given for why cult killer Charles Manson had a swastika carved into his forehead). During the Gallico-Roman period, the spindle-whorl—a swastika

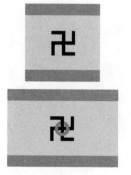

Flags of the Tule Republic.

by any other name—was found on stone pedestals and altars. In England and Scotland, it was known as the *fylfot* (as in "many feet"), and was the embodiment of good fortune and auspicious beginnings. A large mosaic swastika ornamented an ancient synagogue floor in Israel. A copper swastika was unearthed in the nineteenth century at Native American sites: Hopewell Mound in Ross County, Ohio, and Toco Mound in Monroe County, Tennessee.

The swastika was also used by secular organizations. During the nineteenth century, the swastika was a Masonic sign, and Madame Blavatsky adopted it as an emblem of her Theosophist movement. In the 1920s it was selected as the peace symbol for the League of Nations' Vilna Commission; in the 1930s it was a graphic device on the national flags of Estonia, Finland (known as "the Cross of Freedom"), and Latvia. The breakaway state of rebellious Cuna Indians in Panama established the Republic of Tule with a flag that had a counterclockwise swastika emblem. It was used commercially, too, as a trademark on common products and services. And although many of these marks were duly recorded with copyright and trademark registries, no one ever really owned an exclusive copyright to the swastika, which remains in the public domain for anyone to claim.

Desecration of religious icon in Germany, 1960.

Given this auspicious past, the swastika might have remained one of the world's most untarnished, ubiquitous symbols. A graphic symbol is, after all, as weak or as strong as what it represents. And while such an impressive mnemonic device will surely conjure associations that prompt instantaneous recognition, it draws its intensity, first and foremost, from the quality of the thing or idea that it denotes. As a tool of corporate or product identification, for instance, a trademark or logo is neither inherently good nor bad (unless it stems from a malicious or maligning stereotype, like the Frito Bandito); rather, its end use determines how it is perceived. Apart from esoteric and aesthetic qualities, the foundation of a good mark is an exemplary product or service. Conversely, an "award-winning" mark will never compensate for sullied wares and public displeasure.

That for centuries the swastika was not used for harm gave it a positive pedigree. But owing to its vague origin, variegated function, and mystical heritage, it is not surprising that it could be misconstrued or reinterpreted, even in a sinister manner. When in the late nineteenth and early twentieth centuries the swastika was appropriated by esoteric German occultists as their secret signifier, or holy grail containing the mystery of the heavens, the symbol's fate fell into doubt. For this is when the swastika became the sign of an ancient Indo-European elite—an Aryan race. It was believed that the swastika possessed a kind of natural force that comprised a secret heraldry.

Had these cults remained solely on the fringes of German society, it remains uncertain how the swastika would be viewed today by the Western world. But their collective influence had a profound effect on the burgeoning post-war German nationalists, monarchists, and fascists. Even before Germany's defeat by the Allies in the Great War, Aryan supremacy was promoted by the paramilitary, which claimed the swastika as its symbol. As early as 1912, the Reichshammer Bund used the mark as its battle sign. After the armistice, troops of the notorious Freikorp (Free Corps) Ehrhardt Brigade, a uniformed column of army veterans that waged war against the newly founded Weimar Republic, carried the swastika during its street skirmishes. For the Nazis, writes the historian Nicholas Goodrick-Clarke in The Occult Roots of Nazism, there was "a direct line of symbological succession" between the secret societies and the party "in the form of the swastika."

Ultimately, the swastika and Hitler were interchangeable, as exemplified in Leni Reifenstahl's propaganda paean to Nazidom, *Triumph of the Will*. "When

Hitler is absent in Riefenstahl's film," wrote Malcolm Quinn in *The Swastika: Constructing the Symbol* (Routledge, 1997), "his place is taken by the swastika, which, like the image of the Führer, becomes a switching station for personal and national identities." The swastika was indeed such a potent Nazi and national emblem that even half a century after the defeat of the Third Reich, it continues to instill fear and loathing. So enduring is its legacy and, therefore, so offensive is its metaphor that the German government, at the behest of the World War II allies, officially bans all public displays of it. The swastika concentrates such vehemence in its very form that its horror is palpable even in current neo-fascist marks where mere fragments of the swastika are introduced. In fact, the swastika is not simply a vivid reminder of a mournful history, it is an instrument (or at least an accessory) of its depravity.

As such the question of its redemption fosters considerable contention. Redemption of this kind would have to be the function of both official and popular consensus. One might question: Because one man kills another, must all men be deemed killers? Even killers are often given an opportunity to redeem (and cleanse) themselves. Likewise, because a formerly positive icon temporarily represented evil deeds, can it never again

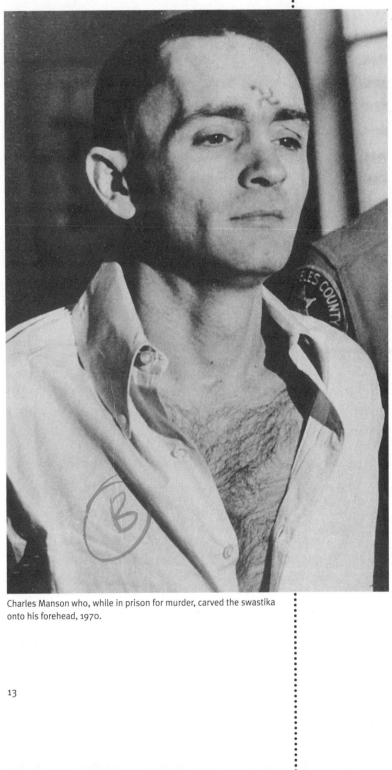

Charles Manson who, while in prison for murder, carved the swastika onto his forehead, 1970.

Above and opposite: poster stamps, c. 1944.

be seen in its original context? Certainly, under the signs of each of the world's great religions, atrocities have occurred. Should the cross, star, and crescent be forbidden? Why was the fasci, Italy's fascist logo (formerly an icon of Imperial Rome) allowed to quietly disappear? And why is the hammer and sickle, which has definitely signified repression for decades longer than the swastika, not as criminally charged?

If the Nazis had not appropriated the swastika, the question of stigma would be moot. But the fact that it was the centerpiece of Nazi pageantry, seal of Nazi officialdom, and mark of Nazi atrocity forever changed its essence. Certain symbols might easily exist ambiguously or with multiple meanings, but ultimately not the swastika. For what once exemplified good fortune now manifests malevolence. What was once innocent is forever guilty.

Some argue today that the swastika was merely a vessel that can be emptied at will. But the swastika is not just any vessel. Nor is it like the marks for Coca-Cola, IBM, Apple, CBS, or other venerable corporate logos that front a company or represent a brand that ultimately rises and falls on popular acceptance. What makes the swastika so consequential is not only that it was the fulcrum of an integrated propaganda machine, but that it is the graphic embodiment of a heinous dogma that encouraged racist-inspired atrocities. Just because the Nazis lost the war does not mean that the symbol is denazified.

The essays in this anthology are a means to address vexing questions about the swastika's place in history, analyzing its present and speculating upon its future. As one who routinely works with graphic images, I find the swastika to be representative of how line, shape, mass, and color can be influential on popular perception when manipulated to serve an idea and promoted vociferously as a brand. Of course, one could select hundreds of different visual forms—from the circle, square, and triangle, to the cross, star, and crescent— to examine how the form of signs and symbols function in the world. But the swastika is the only one among them that triggers the emotions in such a profound way. Regardless of its context, I cringe every time I see the mark, yet I'm continually drawn to it—perhaps in the same way that others have been similarly drawn to it over the millennia.

Buy More War Bonds and Stamps
By E. B. Greenhaw of Artists for Victory ©
TAKE A SMASH AT THE AXIS!
Reproduced by Ever Ready Label Corp., N. Y. C.

chapter two

FROM PREHISTORY
TO HISTORY

The Svastika has a very wide range of distribution, and is found on all kinds of objects. It was used as a religious emblem in India and China at least ten centuries before the Christian era, and is met with on Buddhist coins and inscriptions from various parts of India.

—*Encyclopaedia Britannica*, Eleventh Edition, 1910

Adolf Hitler and the Nazis use the Swastika as their emblem. They claim that it is a pure "Aryan" symbol, that it originated in Europe among the "Aryans," and that it is a special characteristic of the "Aryan" peoples as a whole and of the Germanic people in particular. All available evidence today indicates that these claims are unfounded.

—W. Norman Brown, *The Swastika: A Study of the Nazi Claims of its Aryan Origin*, 1933

The swastika (right) and the suavastika (left).

Long ago man imbued graphic symbols with extraordinary powers representing both god and demon. Born of history, legend, and myth, symbols reflect humankind's innermost beliefs and are key to social ritual. Though created by mortals, the most remarkable symbols never die; civilization's greatest are indeed its oldest. Yet the most sacred, those with meanings indelibly etched into the collective psyche, are not immutable or inviolable.

Few symbols have had as much impact on humankind as the swastika. No other mark has turned up in so many disparate cultures, suggesting some kind of enormous migration or diaspora of peoples joined by a common belief or understanding. This ancient hooked cross gets its name from the Sanskrit word svastika, meaning "well being, good fortune, and luck." Although the first recorded instance of this word is fully two thousand years after the earliest known Indian examples of the symbol, the term, which refers to the Indian mystic figure svastikaya, has probably always meant a "sign of benediction."

The swastika has been traced back to prehistory by many scholars, but no one was more ambitious than Thomas Wilson, who in the late nineteenth century was the curator of the Department of Prehistoric Anthropology at the U.S. National Museum (The Smithsonian Institution, Washington, D.C.). In 1894 he published, with government support, a profusely illustrated, book-length report entitled *The Swastika. The Earliest Known Symbol, And its Migrations; With Observations On The Migration of Certain Industries In Prehistoric Times*. In his preface, Wilson explained that the straight line, the circle, the cross, and the triangle "are simple forms, easily made, and might have been invented and re-invented in every age of primitive man and in every quarter of the globe, each time being an independent invention, meaning much or little, meaning different things among different peoples or at different times

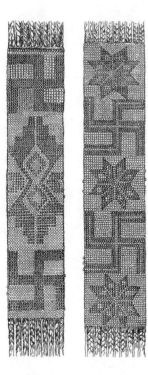

Ceremonial Bead Garters of Sac Indians in Kansas, date unknown. From Report of National Museum, 1894.

among the same people, or they may have not settled or [had a] definite meaning." Conversely, he concluded, the swastika was probably the first symbol to be made with "a definite intention" and a continuous or consecutive meaning, the knowledge of which passed from person to person, from tribe to tribe, from people to people, and from nation to nation, until with possibly changed meanings, it has finally circled the globe." Nonetheless, he offers no definitive conclusion regarding its time or place of origin.

Wilson is certain, however, that the swastika emerged in both hemispheres and throughout virtually every landmass, continent, and country, including the "Extreme orient," "Classical Orient," Africa, "Classical Occident," Mediterranean, Europe, and the Americas. He further analyzed the swastika's application on artifacts—from funeral urns to spears—and classified them according to physical and symbolic properties to determine some logical reason why the swastika has been prevalent in so many disparate cultures for so long. And it remains a mystery.

While numerous interpretations of the swastika differ on this subject, some scholars agree that the model for the symbol must have been an object, known and useful throughout the ancient world. In 1901 an

Swastikas used by the Ashanti from Ghana, date unknown.

Ashanti design cast in bronze, date unknown.

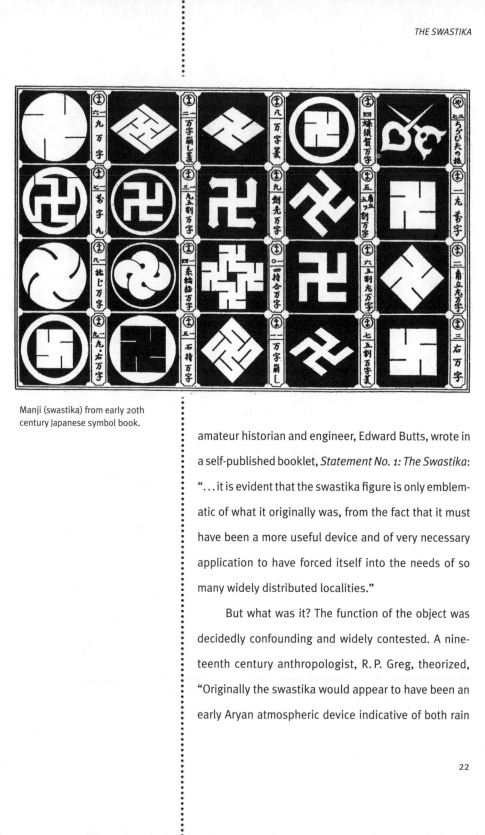

Manji (swastika) from early 20th century Japanese symbol book.

amateur historian and engineer, Edward Butts, wrote in a self-published booklet, *Statement No. 1: The Swastika*: "…it is evident that the swastika figure is only emblematic of what it originally was, from the fact that it must have been a more useful device and of very necessary application to have forced itself into the needs of so many widely distributed localities."

But what was it? The function of the object was decidedly confounding and widely contested. A nineteenth century anthropologist, R. P. Greg, theorized, "Originally the swastika would appear to have been an early Aryan atmospheric device indicative of both rain

22

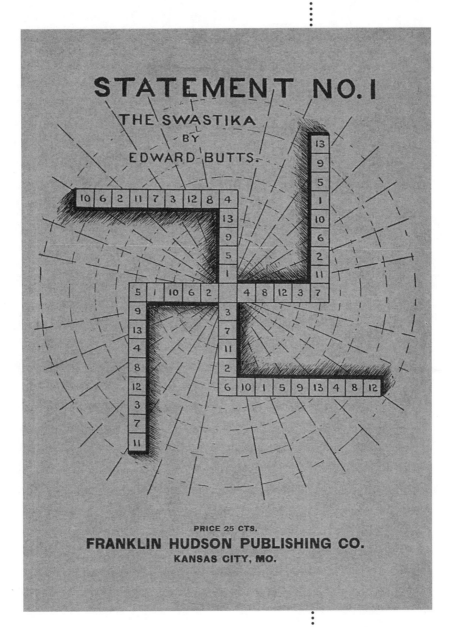

Cover of *Statement
No. 1: The Swastika*,
by Edward Butts, 1921.

Bronze pin-head from the
Caucasus, date unknown.

Mark on black pottery from the
Caucasus, date unknown.

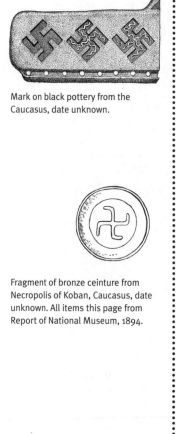

Fragment of bronze ceinture from
Necropolis of Koban, Caucasus, date
unknown. All items this page from
Report of National Museum, 1894.

and lightning." A contemporary, the archeologist Eugene Burnouf, recounted an ancient myth about Arani, an Indian fire stick, which described an instrument made of wood resembling the swastika and used to make fire: "The origin of the sign [swastika] is now easy to recognize. It represents the two pieces of wood which compose The Arani, of which the extremities were bent to be retained by four nails." This theory, however, was refuted by yet another contemporary swastika scholar, Count Goblet d'Alviella, who discounted these presumptions, stating that it would be difficult to start a fire with this particular configuration. Wilson reported on many of these inconclusive theories throughout his book, but he himself concluded that only one thing was certain: "Whatever else the sign Swastika may have stood for... it was always ornamental." Similarly: "Besides everything else... from it have been developed some of the most exquisite running and interlacing designs," wrote Elizabeth E. Goldsmith in *Life Symbols as Related to Sex Symbolism* (G. P. Putnam & Sons, 1924). Some scholars refute Wilson's view, believing that while the swastika may have been ornamental, it was always symbolic as well.

Wilson also uncovered quite a varied assortment of swastika configurations. What he called the "normal" one, with its hooks facing rightward, "is characterized by straight bars of equal thickness throughout, and cross each other at right angles, making four arms of equal size, length, and style." The mirror image of this, with hooks facing leftward, was labeled suavastika by German Indologist Friedrich Max Müller, but Wilson was unable to find corroboration that this term was actually used when the term "swastika" came into currency. Extending the direction debate even further, another nineteenth century "swastikalist," anthropologist, and famous white supremacist Daniel G. Brinton, wrote in a paper titled *The Ta Ki, The Svastika and The Cross* (Mac-Calla & Company, 1889) that the swastika "is a hooked cross or gammated cross... the four arms of equal length, the hook usually pointing from left to right," suggesting that Max Müller's suavastika was, in fact, the "normal" article.

Evidence proves that the swastika was not always perfectly symmetrical or, for that matter, unadorned; sometimes it appeared with dots or points in the corners of the intersections, which causes a deliberate shortening of the hook, and was dubbed Croix Swasticale by a Polish librarian, Michael Zmigrodzki. Yet he also noted that sometimes the hook was shorter for no logical reason. A very common version was a

Spearhead with swastika and triskelion, from Germany, date unknown.

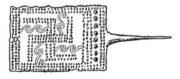

Bronze pin from Bavaria, date unknown. Both objects shown here from Report of National Museum, 1894.

meander pattern with straight ends bent to the right and left, and another one with meandering curves turning right or left. Sometimes these different configurations had the same meaning, other times not.

Nineteenth- and early twentieth-century mystics and scholars went to unusual lengths to explain the arcane significance of the direction of the hooked ends. Some suggest left is man and right is woman, or right is sun and left is sunset—indicating that the right-facing swastika is indeed correct. But wait: "In some localities the right hand motion is considered auspicious and the left hand inauspicious but in general, this distinction is not observed, and both motions are auspicious," wrote W. Norman Brown in *The Swastika: The Study of the Nazi Claims of its Aryan Origin* (Emerson Books, 1933), who adds, "The oldest of the known interpretations may, like the earliest, be only a rationalization of an auspicious character which the symbol had acquired for some reason long since forgotten." In Die Chinesische Monade (Verlag von K. F. Koehler, 1934) written by Kaiser Wilhelm II, the last Imperial German monarch, and published over a decade after the sign was adopted by the Nazis, the swastika is shown in various directions and contours, from the numerous lands in which it was found, without offering a clue to its rightful interpretation. The former

Swastika-like cross, c. 1400s.

Kaiser presumes, but cannot prove, that each iteration had unique positive and negative meanings endemic to these cultures, but what this was is uncertain.

The swastika is generally presumed to have an Aryan/Indian origin. The Aryans, a light-skinned "barbarian" people, according to one theory preferred by later Nazi ideologues, migrated from the north to points east into India and Persia and west towards Greece and Rome, bringing the swastika with them, and so are today considered seminal to the dispersion of the symbol in Asia Minor and from there ultimately to China and Japan. However, some alternative theories suggest that Aryans migrated northward, while others say that Aryans did not exist at all. Whatever the facts, Aryan or Indo-European culture provided the cornerstone for Nazi theories of racial superiority.

One of the theoretical assertions in Wilson's book negates the general use of the term "swastika" because it argues against an Indian origin for the icon, and asserts that it embodies a specific meaning, which "is totally different outside India."

Although "swastika" is the accepted term, it is not the only word used to describe the sign or object. In French it is gammadion, and in German it is Hakenkreuz (or hooked cross). In Britain it was called fylfot from

TOP: Detail of archaic vase found in Cyprus, with serpents, crosses and swastikas, date unknown.

CENTER: Perfume vase from Cyprus, date unknown.

BOTTOM: Detail of vase from Cyprus, date unknown. All images shown here from Report of National Museum, 1894.

TOP: Footprints of Buddha, date unknown.

CENTER: Triskelion on carved wood from Ireland, date unknown. From Report of National Museum, 1894.

BOTTOM: Altar from south of France, date unknown. From Report of National Museum, 1894.

the Scandanavian fower fot, meaning four- or many-footed. The Chinese call it a wan, the Japanese a manji. In Nordic countries it has been called Thor's Hammer (though some scholars argue that the reference is actually to another kind of cross), as well as being known in India as The Footprints of Buddha, owing to the fact that the symbol is etched into a sacred Buddhist stone carving. When Buddha walked, the footprints he left were swastikas. The swastika in this context is Dharma—the symbol of the wheel of the law.

There are significant gaps in the overall history of the swastika, especially at the beginning, yet there are also an extraordinary number of extant examples from all periods and parts of the globe. Many of these have come from archeological excavations during the late nineteenth and early twentieth centuries, and because of them, a provisional history of the symbol's early migration has been attempted (although no one has been able to substantiate the migration theory as opposed to the coincidence theory—i.e., its emergence in many places simultaneously).

According to the migration theory, the swastika's earliest known habitat is a wide territory beginning at the valley of the river Indus in India and extending westward across Persia and Asia Minor to Hissarlik (where

28

the remains of ancient Troy were found) on the shore of the Hellespont. It was there that the famed archeologist Dr. Heinrich Schliemann found many key artifacts during his excavations between 1871 and 1875. However, W. Norman Brown contended that "for combined age, frequency, and perfect execution, the examples from the Indus Valley are the most interesting."

In 1924 the *Archeological Survey of India* announced the first results of excavations it had conducted in the Indus Valley at two sites named Mohenjo- Daro and Harappa, and in 1931 these discoveries were described in three compendious volumes with copious illustration. Among the finds at Mohenjo-Daro and Harappa were many seals with representations of the swastika, which, judging from the evidence, was not anomalous but exceedingly common as decoration. Brown noted that the swastika was among India's "first civilized remains, as early as 2500 B.C., possibly 3000 B.C. and appears in forms perfectly developed, in contrast with slightly older but more primitive and less perfect forms found farther westward." More important, Brown concluded that it existed in India before the arrival of the Aryans. "Like other symbols which the Aryans of India used on coins and stone sculpture, it came to them from non-Aryan predecessors. It was a simple minutia

Cyprian artifacts with swastikas, dates unknown. From Report of National Museum, 1894.

Cyprian artifacts influenced by Phoenician and Greek artisans, dates unknown. From Report of National Museum, 1894.

of the spoils the victors had taken from those they had vanquished."

The swastika was also discovered in the early 1930s in explorations of the ancient civilization in Baluchistan (in central Asia), which is as old as that of the Indus valley. From about the same time, farther to the west in Asia, even more seals were found showing several varieties of the swastika, including the most primitive from around 3000 B.C. Likewise during this period, early painted pottery of Susa, Persia was unearthed. These examples of the swastika and the triskelion (an equally common, three-legged circular symbol) date from before the Indo-European arrival into that region, which historians believe was after 2000 B.C.

The next chronological "stratuth" (as Brown calls it) for the swastika appears at Hissarlik, the site of Homer's Troy, and many older cities that had risen and perished before it. It was here that Schliemann found

30

hundreds of objects, from pottery fragments to terra cotta whorls from around 2000 B.C. (much has been donated to the German National Museum in Berlin), on which swastika signs were common. Recognizing the symbol from pots found near Königswalde on the River Oder in Germany, Schliemann presumed that the swastika was a religious symbol of his Germanic ancestors which linked ancient Teutons, Homeric Greeks, and Vedic India. The Trojan discoveries reaped much publicity throughout Europe and garnered a huge following in Germany, in large part owing to Schliemann's speculations about Aryan ties between Eastern and Western traditions. In fact, the archeologist was himself so captivated by the swastika that he decorated the walls of his own residence in Athens, the Palace of Ilion, with ornaments drawn from his findings.

Hissarlik was a part of the Aegean culture, and throughout the bronze period of that civilization, down to around 1100 B.C., the swastika appears on pottery ornamented with geometrical designs and on other objects. According to Brown (and contrary to Schliemann's assertion), it was at Hissarlik or elsewhere in Asia Minor that the Indo-Europeans may for the first time have met the swastika, but this is only a supposition. It was not long after 2000 B.C. that the Hittites were establishing

Chinese triquetrum swirling design, date unknown.

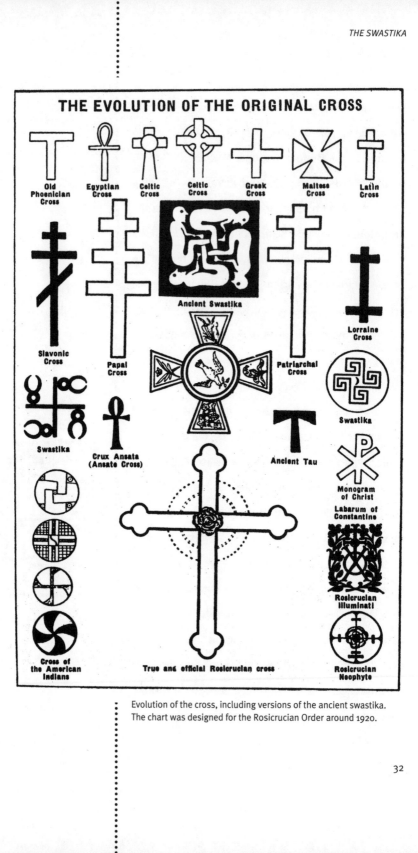

Evolution of the cross, including versions of the ancient swastika.
The chart was designed for the Rosicrucian Order around 1920.

their empire nearby, and it is possible that the other Indo-European elements were then sifting into the population of that region.

Brown contends that Hissarlik may reasonably be considered the point from which the swastika spread to Europe. By way of the Aegean, it went to Greece, and in post-Mycenean times, after the Grecian phase of the Aegean civilization had collapsed, it appeared upon vases in Cyprus, Rhodes, and Athens from the seventeenth century B.C. It is further documented on a funeral car and on the figure of Artemis and other Asiatic deities. It also reached northern Italy, where it was found on certain funerary urns. The great bronze industry of the Aegean, and especially of Hissarlik, sent its wares along the trade routes into Europe. Late in the Bronze period, when ornamented objects appeared in the lower Danube region, the swastika was among the various designs. The Celts who were proficient workers in bronze and gold also used it.

Eventually, the Germans acquired and employed it at the end of the Bronze period. It was abundantly common as ornament, and after the German contact with the Romans (although the Germans believed that the swastika preceded the Roman era), they decorated elaborate plaques with it. Brown chronicles that in at

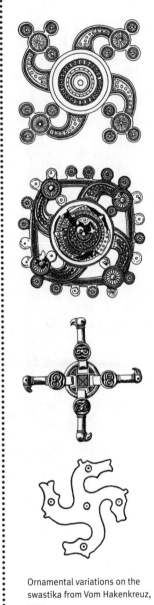

Ornamental variations on the swastika from *Vom Hakenkreuz*, 1921.

Fragment of artifact published in findings of Dr. Heinrich
Schliemann's excavation of Troy, 1885.

least one instance, the swastika and other symbols appeared with a male figure who "is possibly a god, but certainly not the Christian God." The Gallic peoples employed it, and during the Gallico-Roman period in Aquitania and Britain, it is found on altars, where it is associated with the thunderbolt which in Scandinavia is said to represent the god Thor.

The swastika was found over such a large part of the globe because it was a fundamental shape and design. Nonetheless, some scholars (and particularly German ones) argued that it did not appear in parts of the civilized world. For example, Brown wrote that "Egypt seems to have been without it until very late, when Greece had arisen. Ancient Assyria and Palestine, as far as I know, were also without it... Although by 2000 B.C. it extended across to the Hellespont, it passed to the north of the great Semitic territory and missed that people. The Jews did not use it. Early Christianity seems not to have known it. The Christians used the swastika only after their religion was well established in Europe." And yet evidence is offered to the contrary. In 1921, a German author, Jörg Lechler, edited an issue of Vorzeit, an journal of German history, on the Hakenkreuz that showed illustrations of the swastika's inclusion on Christian churches and abbeys. More surprising, exca-

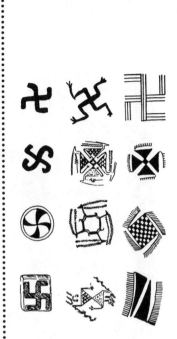

Swastikas from Africa documented by Kaiser Wilhelm II in 1934.

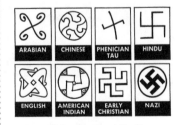

Comparative chart issued by the United States government in 1940s.

Detail of mosaic floor from Ein-
Gedi synagogue, date unknown.

vations during the later twentieth century revealed that ancient synagogues—Sussiya in North Africa, Eshtamoa and Ein-Gedi in Palestine—featured decorative swastika mosaics from the mid-sixth century A.D. The swastika at Ein-Gedi even had greater prominence than those found in other synagogues as an icon that stood alone, not part of a larger decorative design. Hershel Shanks notes in *Judaism in Stone: The Archaeology of Ancient Synagogues* (Harper and Row, 1979) that prior to the Nazi era, swastikas were not confined to ancient synagogues either: "After Hitler came to power congregants of the Emmanuel Synagogue of Hartford, Connecticut discovered to their horror that the synagogue vestibule had been paved with a mosaic containing several swastikas. The mosaic pavement was promptly paved out."

Before the time of Columbus, the swastika was found in northern, central, and southern America in many variant forms. It is possible that it may have originated on this continent independently of Europe and Asia; on the other hand, it may have migrated here. Early contacts between Asia and America are now accepted, but their nature and extent are uncertain. And such is the nature of this unique diaspora.

When addressing what the swastika ultimately became, it is important to reiterate that it was not invented

Detail of artifact published in findings of Dr. Heinrich Schliemann's excavation of Troy, 1885.

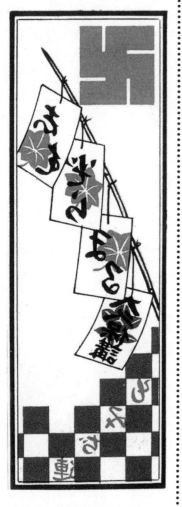

Japanese advertising banner, 1930s.

by the Indo-Europeans. Brown, whose text was designed to refute Nazi claims, was emphatic that the people among whom it first appeared were what he called the Japhetic and Indus Valley peoples. "Whatever these various peoples were, they were not Indo Europeans; and the Indo Europeans, as far as our evidence indicates, did not know the swastika until a thousand years after the time of its earliest preserved specimens." The Indo-Europeans may have had it in Asia Minor very early in the second millennium B.C. or in upper Iraq or Persia shortly afterwards, and again in India shortly after that. But the Germans do not seem to have had the symbol until the first millennium B.C.

Yet after Schliemann's discovery and subsequent theory concerning the swastika's Aryan roots—and regardless of the questions of origin posed by objective scientists—the sign's "official" history was written in concert with the myths of Aryanism. By the late nineteenth and early twentieth century, German racist mystics and occultists adopted the swastika as their sacred icon of racial purity and invented a heritage and lore to support it. At this moment the swastika's transformation begins.

chapter three

FOLK, MYTH,
OCCULT, NAZIS

[We must fight] until the swastika rises victoriously out of the icy darkness...

—Rudolf von Sebottendorff, c.1918

We believe that someday Heaven will unite all Germans in one Reich, not under the Soviet star or the Jewish Star of David, but under the Swastika...

— Adolf Hitler, May 1,1923

I see in the flags not only a symbol of the Nazi movement but also the earthly form in which the Eternal God has revealed Himself.

— Baldur von Schirach, Leader of the Hitler Youth Organization, 1937

The four intersecting legs of the swastika could very well symbolize folklore, mythology, occultism, and ideology, for these underscored its significance during the early twentieth century. Adoption of the swastika for the Nazi Party was based solely upon the debatable theory that the symbol was an Aryan sign representing a racial bond between Teutonic and Eastern, particularly Indian, civilizations. The Nazis did not select the swastika for its striking graphic quality alone. In a real sense it was chosen for them by the pseudoscientists, folklorists, and occultists who believed that it was a sacred totem of Aryan or Indo-European culture. As descendants of Aryan tribes ruled by great gods and demons, German

Calendar wheel in form of swastika presents the four seasons, date unknown.

mystics transformed the swastika into a symbol of racial purity and superiority.

During the late nineteenth century, the princely states that comprised Germania were forged into a unified nation with imperialistic aspirations wherein fervent nationalism and Pan-Germanic ideology gained

42

acceptance among certain sectors of the population. Racial and political theories that emerged from these quarters were hammered into doctrines fostered by secret occult orders, as well as radical political organizations. Certain ritualistic aspects of the nascent Nazi movement derived from cult groups such as the Germanen Order, The Thule Society, and The New Templars, each of which embraced the mystical symbolism ascribed to the swastika.

The swastika's metamorphosis began innocently enough with Dr. Schliemann's Trojan excavation in 1874. But once he and others used the symbol to validate German claims of Aryan ascendancy, a sinister dogma began to take hold. Owing to the magnitude of the discovery—akin in its day to landing a man on the moon—Germans hungered for further insights into their supremacist heritage. A prodigious number of books, pamphlets, and lectures touted German racial dominance, and many of these ideas were formulated by otherwise serious scientists who advanced racialism and eugenics as part of the natural order. Owing to its prominence as an ancient icon, the swastika soon embodied many of these ideas. Therefore, in the wake of World War I, by the time the Nazi party became a political influence, the symbol was already on the road to ignominy.

Logo for Thule Society, 1919.

Schliemann's renown as an archeologist gave credence to his obsession with the swastika's role as an Aryan symbol. According to Nicolas Goodrick-Clarke in *Hitler's Priestess: Savitri Devi, the Hindu-Aryan Myth, and Neo-Nazism* (New York University Press, 1998), Schliemann planted a seed in the European mind "that the swastika was a uniquely Aryan religious symbol whose spatial distribution mapped the racial continuities of the ancient West and the mysterious East." Although Schliemann did not advocate rabid anti-Semitic views himself, his collaborator, Eugene Burnouf was a known anti-Semite. Burnouf asserted in his writing that the swastika was never accepted by the Jews (later excavations proved this to be false), and he used this assertion as a rationale for its role as an anti-Semitic sign. Others who embraced Schliemann's discoveries and promoted swastika scholarship were openly racist as well. Professor Friedrich Max Müller made no secret of his racist interpretations: For him, the swastika was not a benign sign of rebirth, but the mark of the supreme Aryan god, which would reestablish itself as a symbol of power in Germany and throughout Europe. Michael Zmigrodzki, a Polish librarian and avowed anti-Semite, mounted an exhibition of swastika artifacts at the Paris Exposition of 1889, but before that, in 1886, he lectured before

Shield found on Abbey of Lambach, 1869.

Poster for Germanen Order, c. 1914.

a congress of scientists and "swastikaphiles" on the Aryan virtues of the form. That same year he published a racist tract, *Die Mutter bei den Völkern des arischen Stammes*, which further underscored the anti-Semitic symbolism of the sign by focusing on Aryans as a pure race that excluded Semitic interbreeding. In 1891, Ernst Ludwig Krause wrote *Tuisko-Land, der arischen Stämme und Götter Urheimat*, which unequivocally introduced the swastika as a mark of völkisch or folk nationalism, which was also resolutely anti-Semitic.

Racialist pseudoscience provided only one of the thrusts for the swastika myth. It was further popularized by occultism, which had an increased presence in Germany and throughout Western Europe during the late nineteenth and early twentieth centuries. One of the most significant of the swastika's advocates was Madame Helena Petrovna Blavatsky, the Russian-born medium and founder, in 1875, of the Theosophical Society, which integrated aspects of spiritualism, gnosticism, the Kabbala, and Freemasonry with Eastern wisdom, including Hinduism and Buddhism. Although the Kabbala was part of Jewish mysticism, Blavatsky refuted such claims by asserting its ancient German mystical roots. In her seminal book, *The Secret Doctrine* (1888), she wrote of human evolution progressing through seven races,

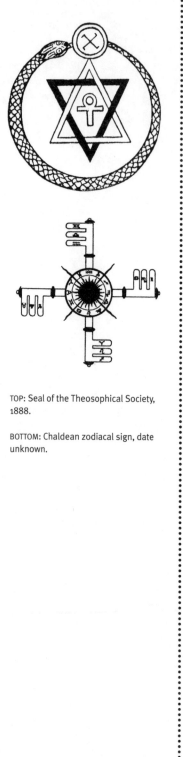

TOP: Seal of the Theosophical Society, 1888.

BOTTOM: Chaldean zodiacal sign, date unknown.

the fifth one being the Aryan race. Consistent with this concept is the importance she gives to the swastika as a mystical touchstone, which incidentally appeared on her own brooch, in the seal of the Theosophical Society, and on the title page of her books. While Theosophy taught a decidedly universal view of life, Blavatsky's inclusion of the Aryans and the swastika in her teachings had an influence on German and Austrian secret mystical (and racist) societies at the turn of the century.

Secret societies were common throughout Europe, and one of the largest and most venerable was the Freemasons. This order of builders and engineers (among other craftsmen) claimed that its initiates dated back to the architects of the pyramids in ancient Egypt. The Freemasons developed secret signs and symbols used to distinguish levels of expertise in order to identify masters from apprentices. Among the litany of Mason's marks found in the *Royal Masonic Cyclopaedia* (1877), the swastika was called the Hermetic Cross (Hermeticism was a form of Gnostic Christianity) and was "used only by members of the Governing Body of the Order of Ishmael, Esau, Reconciliation, and Expiation." It was further referred to as the "Jaina Cross," as used "by several orders, and occurs constantly as a mark of Masonic importance in several of the abbeys of Great

Britain... It has a variety of significations, and was adopted by the sect of the Jains as a specific symbol." (Jainism is an Indian religion that believes in the purity of the soul and abstinence from killing living things.) German racial occultists, however, abhorred Freemasonry, not just for retaining the swastika in a non-Aryan form, but because they asserted that the liberal order was dominated by Jews (which was among the reasons that the Nazis outlawed Freemasonry). Yet the Freemason paradigm—through which initiates and members were prohibited entry to graduated levels unless they possessed the keys of knowledge and experience—appealed to German occultists, who instituted strict entry requirements based on racial proscription.

"The mystical and the occult were taken both as an explanation and as a solution to man's alienation from modern society, culture, and politics," wrote George L. Mosse in *The Fascist Revolution* (Howard Fertig, 1999). "Not by everyone, of course, but by a minority that found a home in the radical right." Numerous mystic and völkisch nationalist orders and lodges emerged throughout Germany and Austria after the turn of the century, conforming to "secret traditions" that wed racialism and Gnostic mysticism (also known as "secret sciences"). These ideologies were based on the exis-

Drawing for Nazi poster by Adolf Hitler, c. 1933.

Badges of the Nazi party, 1933.

tence of dark cosmic life forces and underscored by the glories of a romantic Aryan past that went counter to the materialism and urbanism of the Modern age. "Occultism was invoked to endorse the reducing validity of an obsolescent and precarious social order," writes Nicolas Goodrick-Clarke in *The Occult Roots of Nazism* (NYU Press, 1982). Each of these orders employed the swastika as a symbol of Aryan transcendence.

These cults were usually led by charismatic figures who solely developed a legacy of myth and dogma. Viennese-born Guido Von List (1848–1919) was the earliest and most influential "mystogogue," and his teaching was taken seriously by certain historical societies. List subscribed to Wotanism, a pre-Christian pagan sect, and he established the Armanen Brotherhood, which he claimed was derived from a Germanic tribe known as the Herminones that included a race of highly developed clairvoyant Germanic priests. List asserted that he was, in fact, the last survivor of this race who possessed the supernatural power to recall the past, which was quite useful in validating the mythology that he professed. "List believed that the Aryan past was the 'genuine' manifestation... It was the closest to nature and therefore farthest removed from artificiality—from materialism and rationalism," states Mosse. Indeed,

List's most viable mystical tool was the ancient Teutonic language known as Runes, which he reinvented as a supressed, symbolic lexicon, on which he based his "Runic knowledge."

The Armanen was the source of the secret, northern Runic language (or "holy-signs") of sharp, linear marks used for writing and carving and known only to believers. The Runes are mentioned as early as 98 A.D. by Tacitus, who described Germans as making these marks on branches and using them for divination. Each Rune had its own name and signification and possessed a symbolism beyond its phonetic values. As such, runes were used in the casting of spiritual signs. In List's most well-known book, *The Secret of the Runes* (1908), he provided a veritable Rosetta stone for initiates to his List Society. According to List, the swastika, which he calls the fryfos, or hook-cross, was the eighteenth rune. In the actual Runic language, however, nothing related to a swastika exists. In List's invented liturgy, however, it was one of the Armanen's holiest symbols because it represented the sun. In Armanen dogma, the solar symbol held the key to the ancient secret science. In völkisch racism, one premise of racial superiority distinguished sun-worshipers from others (i.e., the völk from urban Jews). List noted that a substitute for the eighteenth rune was the "ge" or "gibor"

Cover of Der Adler, an official German army publication, 1944.

or "Gibor-Alter"—God the All-Begetter (the primal word "gi" or "ge," he wrote, stands for "arising" or "being"), which accounts for why the swastika has been called the Gibor rune. (Incidentally, the double "sig"—or "Seig"—rune was later adopted as the mark of the SS.) During a summer solstice celebration in 1875, List reportedly buried wine bottles arranged in the shape of a swastika, which was the first known "modern" demonstration of the symbol in Germany. Decades later, after the Anschlus (or Nazi annexation) of Austria, Hitler wanted to exhume this "first swastika."

List believed that the swastika, as well as other bent crosses, were unique to Aryan heraldry as the repository of energy. Eventually, it was a common fashion around the turn of the century for youth groups as well as occultists to wear the swastika symbol much in the same way the Egyptian Ankh was popular among hippies during the 1960s. List further advocated a Gothic revival in Germany, which was counter to William Morris' Gothic aestheticism in England (which underscored his special brand of liberalism and socialism). For List, Gothic architecture contained ancient secrets with roots in Armenism. Accordingly, he also encouraged the use of spiky Fraktur type in his publications, because it evoked the glorified past.

Poster for Hitler Youth, c. 1938.

Hitler Youth leader speaking before
meeting of graphic artists, 1938.

Jörg Lanz von Liebenfels (1874–1954), the pseud-
onym for Adolf Josef Lanz, a Christian Gnostic and former
novitiate of the Cistercian order, was a List acolyte and
occult leader in his own right. In 1892, he experienced a
revelation that hardened his Manichaean worldview of
the violent opposition between blue-eyed, blond Aryans
and inferior races. In 1899 he founded The Order of the
New Templar, which devoted itself to pure racial breed-
ing and promoted an "Ario-Christian doctrine" that is

formulated on a battle between the forces of good and evil—the Aryan "ace-men" as warriors against submen and racial inferiors, with Frauja (another name for Jesus Christ) as the savior. "Templar" was an organization founded during the Crusades, which occultists argue was a religious and military order working to expunge evil from the world. In the occultist mind, the Templars still existed to carry out the same goals. Lanz established his secret order in Castle Werfenstein and, influenced by List's writings about the eighteenth rune, Lanz designed an emblem for its flag that contained a red swastika and blue lilies against a golden background. He hoisted the flag for the first time on Christmas day. In 1905 he inaugurated *Ostara: Briefbücherei der blonden Mannes-rechtler* (Newsletter of the Blond Fighters for the Rights of Men), a profoundly anti-Semitic journal, which debated the metaphysics of race and offered such wisdom as blond men are the creators and preservers of civiliza-tion. Ostara featured a trademark of a knight in hooded robes decorated with numerous swastikas. In 1916, Lanz coined the term Arisophy to describe the pseudoscience of Aryanism. Ostara included articles on racial superiority based on his 1904 tract called *Theozoology, or the Lore of Sodom's Apes and Gods' Electron*, wherein he espouses enslaving inferior races and limiting their procreation

Logo for *Ostara* magazine, c. 1905.

Swastika as national flag and global power, 1937.

on the grounds of economic and social scientific ratio-
nales. He further advocated keeping "brood-mothers"
in convents to be impregnated by Aryan "stud-males."
As Goodrich-Clarke observes, "The similarity between
Lanz's proposals and later practices of [Reichführer
Heinrich] Himmler's SS Lebensborn maternity organization, and the Nazi plans for the disposal of the Jews"
was not coincidence. Various biographies of Adolf Hitler
indicate that he was a frequent reader of Ostara and, at
least in the early years, shared some of Lanz's beliefs.
He also reportedly visited Lanz to obtain missing issues
in the series. Regardless, after the Nazis came to power,
Lanz's writing was banned, perhaps as a way for Hitler
to disavow the fact that he was influenced by anything
other than his own immaculate conceptions.

The Germanen Order, which ran from 1912 to 1922,
is the völkisch occult group most closely linked to the
nascent Nazi party and doubtless inspired its adoption
of the swastika. After 1916 its newsletter, the Allgemeine
Ordens-Nachrichten displayed a curved swastika superimposed on a cross as its mark (later advertisements in
the publication sold rings and pendants with swastika
designs). The founders of the Order, Theodor Fritsch
(who published the anti-Semitic Hammer), Philipp
Stauff, Henrich Kräger, and Herman Pohl were rabid

anti-Semites who warned that Jewry was an international conspiratorial movement which, among its other crimes, "polluted" the Freemasons. The order was founded as an alternative to (yet on the model of) the Freemasons in order to exclude and plot against Jewish elements in German life. The Wotan lodge was the first of the Germanen secret societies. As initiation rights, Order members adorned Knights' robes topped by helmets with Wotan's horns and engaged in candlelight ceremonies. Such ceremonies are the precursor of similar Nazi pagan pageants, where Germanen brothers lined up to make a human sign of the swastika.

Following World War I, the Bavarian chapter of the Order was renamed the Thule Society to avoid the detection of republicans and other unwelcome initiates. Ultima Thule was a reference to a long-lost advanced civilization which came from Iceland, which List asserted was an outpost of the Germanic priesthood. In 1918, the Thule Society was taken over by Baron Rudolf von Sebottendorff, a self-styled noble who published a periodical called Runen that appealed to new members through a marriage of Aryan wisdom and unbridled hatred for Jews. Given its relationship to the other secret societies, Thule introduced a new emblem comprised of a long dagger superimposed on a curved swastika sunwheel.

Architectural ornaments in Nuremberg, 1936.

Logo for Reichsmusikkammer Bund,
c. 1937.

Thule attracted right-wing members who, enraged by the overthrow of the monarchist Bavarian government in 1918 by Socialists (some of whom were Jews), sought a means to violently unseat the new regime. Immediately following the takeover, Sebottendorff pledged his loyalty to Germany, the swastika, and destruction of the enemy. In one of his speeches he introduced an additional symbolic icon to the language of völkisch occultism—the Ar-rune, which signifies Aryan, primal fire, the sun, and the eagle. "And the eagle," he announced, "is the symbol of the Aryans. In order to depict the eagle's capacity for self-immolation by fire, it is colored red. From today on our symbol is the red eagle, which warns us that we must die in order to live." Sebottendorff appears to have added even more to the liturgy: He instituted as the order's greeting Sieg Heil (Glory [Victory] Hail), which later became the primary Nazi salute, and he popularized the Führerprinzip, or leader cult, that demands blind obedience to a master who possess the secret knowledge. In this sense the Thulists awaited the greatest symbolic embodiment of all: a Messiah. Indeed one of its leading members, Dietrich Eckart, promoted Adolf Hitler as that superbeing.

By 1914, when Germany was consumed by a world war, the swastika as a nationalist emblem was already adopted by the Wandervogel, a militarist German youth movement, many of whose members became army officers. With Germany's ignominious defeat in 1918, numerous veterans—some members of the secret orders and lodges—believing that Jews, Communists, and republicans betrayed them and profited off defeat, banded together into paramilitary organizations known as Freikorps (Free Corps) or Stahlhelm (Steel Helmet) dedicated to fighting a civil war for the Fatherland against the perfidious traitors. They were frequently employed by the Reichswehr (German army) to carry out illicit acts of violence against its socialist and Communist enemies. The most infamous of these was known as the Ehrhardt Brigade, which in 1919 participated in the liberation of Munich from the Communists and wore the Hakenkreuz on their steel helmets, marking the first time the swastika was associated with a military force in opposition to the Weimar Republic.

The frequent use of the swastika as badge and flag by occult and political groups leading up to the creation in 1918 of the German Workers Party (DAP), renamed in 1920 the National Socialist German Workers Party (NSDAP or Nazis), explains why it was adopted by this movement. But the manner of its adoption has been veiled by the mythology created by and for Adolf Hitler

Nazi party standard, c. 1935.

Graphic artists in the Hitler Youth, c. 1938.

in an attempt to purge any outside influence from his past. Although he did not found the Nazis (at the outset he was its propaganda chief), his gift for hypnotic public speaking thrust him into the forefront of the party's activities. Therefore, as the movement's most compelling draw, he was able to dictate terms that in 1920 propelled him into the leadership position. From that point on the truth regarding the swastika is somewhat hazy.

"It was the strength of fascism in general that it realized, as other political movements and parties did not, that with the nineteenth century Europe had entered a visual age, the age of political symbols, such as the national flag or the national anthem—which, as instruments of mass politics in the end proved more effective than any didactic speeches," writes George L. Mosse. And since Hitler was a wannabe architect, painter, and dabbler in commercial art, as leader of his movement he chose to be its art director and image manipulator. His understanding of symbolism, propaganda, and design was influenced by others, but he set forth distinct guidelines for the rightness of form. In excerpts from *Mein Kampf* (My Struggle) devoted to symbolism, he wrote in stupifyingly formal prose replete with euphemisms and epithets that enforced his own self-styled heroism, yet convincingly argued the need for a powerful symbol/emblem/logo for

Hitler Youth in arts and crafts class, c. 1938.

his nascent party. "The lack of such symbols," he wrote, "had not only disadvantages for the moment, but it was unbearable for the future. The disadvantages were above all that the party members lacked every outward sign of their belonging together, while for the future it was unbearable to lack an emblem that had the character of a symbol of the movement and that as such could be put up in opposition to the International [the Communists]." Hitler recalled the first time he witnessed a large Com-

Saul Steinberg, Untitled (Hitler drawing faulty swastikas), 1946.
© 2000, estate of Saul Steinberg/Art-
ists Rights Society (ARS), New York,
© Corbis.

munist party rally where he saw a sea of red on flags,
scarves, and flowers among the one hundred thousand in
attendance. "I personally could feel and understand how
easily a man of the people succumbs to the suggestive
charm of such a grand and massive spectacle."

Similar to the earlier occult view, Hitler's vision
of the German Reich was of a rebirth and return to real
and imagined past glories, contingent on the destruction
of the enemy within—including the bourgeoisie, Jews,
and Communists. With this as his goal he described
in Mein Kampf his quest to find the perfect symbol for
the party and briefly chronicled his invitation for new

62

Election poster for Nazi party, 1932.

ideas among party members: "Suggestions were made from all sides which, however, were better meant than they were successful," wrote Hitler. "For the new flag had to be as much a symbol of our own fight as on the other hand it had to have an effect as great as that of a poster... In hundreds of thousands of cases, an effective emblem can give the first impetus for the interest in a movement." In his role as art director, Hitler was never satisfied with the results of this open competition, but he nonetheless attempted to be somewhat objective: "I had to reject, without exception, the numerous designs that in those days were handed in by circles of the young

Der Reichstag in Flammen!

Von Kommunisten in Brand gesteckt!

So würde das ganze Land aussehen, wenn der Kommunismus und die mit ihm verbündete Sozialdemokratie auch nur auf ein paar Monate an die Macht kämen!

Brave Bürger als Geiseln an die Wand gestellt! Den Bauern den roten Hahn aufs Dach gesetzt!

Wie ein Aufschrei muß es durch Deutschland gehen:

Zerstampft den Kommunismus!
Zerschmettert die Sozialdemokratie!

Wählt **Hitler 1** Liste

Election poster, 1932.

movement and that mostly had placed the swastika on the old flag. I myself—as leader—did not want to come forth immediately with my own sketch, as it was quite possible that someone else would produce one that was just as good or even better."

Although Hitler designed maquettes for many of the party's posters and emblems using swastika motifs, and even sketched a curved sun wheel version as a possible flag, in fact, the adopted form was ostensibly designed by Dr. Friedrich Krohn, a dentist from Starnberg and a Thulean member of the DAP known for his scholarship in völkisch symbology. Hitler never acknowledges him by name in Mein Kampf, but about Krohn's design, he wrote that it "was not bad at all, and besides that approached my own design very closely, except that it had the mistake that the swastika was composed in a white circle with curved hooks. Meanwhile, I myself, after innumerable attempts, had put down a final form: a flag with a background of red, with a white circle, and in its center, a black swastika. And this then was kept." Actually, in 1919, Krohn wrote a report titled "Is the swastika suitable as the symbol of the National Socialist Party?" in which he proposed the left-handed version (clockwise as opposed to counterclockwise) as the party's new mark and the color combination that

Hitler took credit for. Hitler's major contribution was to reverse the direction of the swastika. According to an Associated Press story dated October 1944, Hitler preferred this direction because he had seen the swastika on the coat of arms of Theodore Hagen at the Abbe of Lambach. Other speculations suggest more mystical inspirations. Regardless, Hitler's "design" decision was accepted without debate.

At the time, much controversy surrounded the Weimar government's rejection of the black, white, and red colors of the imperial German flag and its adoption of a new republican national banner with red, black, and gold color bands (although the imperial flag continued to be flown on military vessels). Like many rightists, Hitler was incensed by the republic and obsessed by its color symbolism. In turn, he wrote a brief color analysis of his own in Mein Kampf that reads like a paper on semiotics: "White is not a color that carries people away. It is suitable for associations of chaste virgins, but not for the overpowering movement of a revolutionary time... [Black] is also not thrilling enough... White and blue was out of the question, despite the wonderful effect from the aesthetic point of view, as the color of a German individual State and of a political orientation directed at particularistic narrow-mindedness that did not enjoy the

Political poster with symbol of Groß-deutchland, 1938.

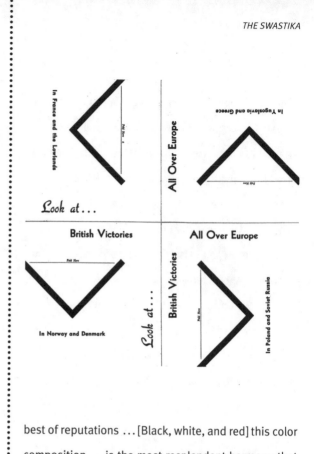

German propaganda leaflet used in war against the British, 1941.

best of reputations ... [Black, white, and red] this color composition ... is the most resplendent harmony that exists." For Hitler the marriage of color and form were inextricably wed to his ideology: "As National Socialists we see our program in our flag. In the red we see the social idea of the movement, in the white the national idea, in the swastika the mission of the fight for the victory of the idea, of creative work, which in itself is and always will be anti-Semitic."

Hitler took ownership of the swastika with the assertion that "In the midsummer of 1920, the new flag appeared in public for the first time ... No one had ever

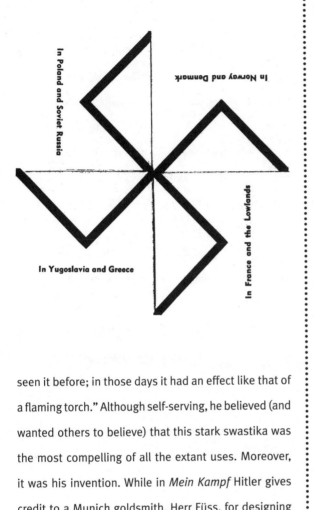

In Poland and Soviet Russia

In Norway and Denmark

In Yugoslavia and Greece

In France and the Lowlands

seen it before; in those days it had an effect like that of a flaming torch." Although self-serving, he believed (and wanted others to believe) that this stark swastika was the most compelling of all the extant uses. Moreover, it was his invention. While in *Mein Kampf* Hitler gives credit to a Munich goldsmith, Herr Füss, for designing the party's badge, he does not credit Wilhelm Deffke, a leading German logo and trademark designer of the age, for having apparently refined and stylized a version of the swastika prior to 1920. According to the designer's former assistant, Deffke was branded a "cultural Bolshevist" by the Nazis, but in a later biographical note

Nazi standards used at Nuremberg rally, 1935.

on her employer, she wrote: "Deffke came across a representation of the ancient Germanic sun wheel on which he worked to redefine and stylize its shape. Later on this symbol appeared in a brochure which he had published, they [The Nazis] chose it as their symbol but reversed it... Needless to say, this was done without any thought of copyright or compensation to the 'cultural Bolshevist.'"

Regardless of who contributed what to the image, the swastika would not have been used if Hitler did not want it, nor would it have been applied so effectively and systematically (mostly through the offices of Dr. Josef Goebbels, the minister of propaganda, and the graphic pageantry of architect Albert Speer). Even the most vociferous opponents of Nazism agree that Hitler's "identity system" is the most ingeniously consistent graphic program ever devised. That he succeeded in transmuting an ancient symbol that had such a long-lasting historical significance into one even more indelible—and in such a comparatively short span of time—is attributable to his complete mastery of the design and propaganda processes.

Josef Goebbels's May 19, 1933 decree, the "Law for Protection of National Symbols," insured the transcendence of the swastika by preventing its unauthorized commercial use (and yet it appeared in or as every conceivable permutation, from cuff links to Christmas tree stands). That same year the Nazi government decreed that on all public buildings in Germany "the old black, white, and red colors of the imperial regime shall fly side by side with the Nazi swastika." And this signified what Hitler termed in a speech "the puissant rebirth of the German nation." The *New York Times* reported, however, that "In accepting the imperial flag and the Nazi hooked-cross banner, President von Hindenburg accepts the political triumph of the parties of which they are the symbol, but his oath of allegiance to the Republic still stands inviolate." Nonetheless, the swastika was rising to ever-greater heights in the symbology of the German nation.

By 1935, Nazi power was absolute, Hitler wielded dictatorial control, and swastikas flew on all properties in Germany and abroad. But in New York City the symbol was so negatively charged that on September 1, 1935, it was banned from flying in at least two hotels where German diplomats were residing. And although it was hoisted on three ocean liners docked in New York Harbor on September 5, 1935, over two thousand demonstrators ("Reds" as the *Times* labeled them) tore down the swastika ensign from the North German Lloyd

Election poster, c. 1932.

(REG. TRADE MARK)

"Fight for Freedom" logo, a British anti-Nazi campaign, c. 1941.

S. S. Bremen's mast. After the melee the perpetrators were arrested, but at their arraignment Louis B. Brodsky, the city court magistrate, compared the swastika to the black flag of a pirate ship and added: "It may well be that the flying of this emblem in New York Harbor was, rightly or wrongly, regarded by these defendants and others of our citizenry as a gratuitously brazen flaunting of an emblem which symbolizes all that is antithetical to American ideals of the God-given and inalienable rights of people to life, liberty and the pursuit of happiness... A revolt against civilization—in brief, if I may borrow a biological concept, an atavistic throwback to pre-medieval, if not barbaric, social and political conditions." The German ambassador in Washington demanded an official State Department apology, but since the swastika was not the national flag, the incident was handled by lower-level officials. This seems to have been the propaganda opportunity Hitler needed. Citing an "insult" to the German people on September 15, 1935, he enacted the first of the Nuremberg laws making the swastika Germany's only national flag. The law read as follows:

Article I: The Reich's colors are black, white and red.

Article II: The Reich's national flag is the swastika flag. It is its commercial flag at the same time.

Article III: The Führer Chancellor will designate the form

of the Reich war flag and the Reich official flag.

Article IV: The Reich's Minister of the Interior will

determine, in so far as the competence of the Reich

War Minister is not involved, the carrying out of and

supplementing of this law with necessary legal and

administrative measures.

On the same day, the next laws to be approved at

this, the first session of the Reichstag ever convened in

Nuremberg rather than Berlin, were the infamous Jew-

ish laws, which in addition to stripping away the rights

of citizenship from the Jews, prohibited them from ever

flying the national flag.

Hitler further consolidated the power of the swas-

tika on November 7, 1935 with the introduction of a new

war (or military) flag, which he personally designed.

According to the *New York Times*, "The new war flag, it

was officially revealed today, definitely puts the German

armed forces under the swastika cross, although some

concessions have been made to the old army colors

and symbols." The new banner was red with a cross

consisting of alternating black and white bars extending

through the length and breadth but dominated by a big

swastika in the central circle. Although veterans were

Swastika souvenir, c. 1940.

Political poster, c. 1933.

reportedly resentful of the nazified banner, popular interest was otherwise reported as mild. But for the recruits who took their oath under the unfurled flag, Hitler made certain that the symbolism could not be ignored. "Soldiers of the armed forces!" he exclaimed. "The swastika cross shall be for you a symbol of the nation's unity and purity, an emblem of the National Socialist Weltanschuung [world view] and a pledge for the Reich's freedom and strength." On the same day, Nazi courts fined Father Albert Coppenrath, a priest in Berlin, fifty marks for failing to fly the swastika on his church, and fourteen other priests were summoned by the secret political police on the charge of disobeying the decree requiring all churches to show swastikas on all public occasions. In keeping with the symbol's role as a monumental German icon, the largest swastika still extant, according to Robert N. Proctor in *The Nazi War on Cancer* (Princeton University Press, 1999), is a grove of conifers planted in a field near Berlin in the form of a one-hundred-meter Hakenkreuz. "More than sixty years after planting, the design emerges every autumn, as the surrounding deciduous trees change colors. It is visible from the air."

In only a few short years, the swastika was transformed from an occult talisman into national icon. But the Nazi defeat in 1945 and the horrific evidence of widespread atrocities ultimately made the swastika synonymous with evil, a fact that did not go unnoticed in Allied military and political circles. Given the swastika's significance, under denazification the prohibition of the symbol was absolute. The Times reported on April 28, 1945, that prisoners of war in the United States were forbidden to use the right-arm fascist salute, and "All German flags on which the swastika appears will be confiscated and prisoners will be prohibited from having in their possession or displaying Nazi emblems, insignia or pictures." Similarly, during the occupation of Germany, "Law No. 154, OMGUS: The Elimination and Prohibition of Military Training. July 14, 1945" declared: "The use of military or Nazi uniforms, insignia, flags, banners or tokens and the employment of distinctive Nazi or military salutes, gestures or greetings are hereby prohibited and declared illegal..."

When the Americans occupied Germany in 1945, most of the "official art" of the Reich, including paintings and posters in the National Socialist heroic style, was sent to the United States and hidden from view. A committee of art historians and government officials decided that "no work that depicts a swastika or any other Nazi insignia should be returned to Germany."

Cover of *Hitler Terror*, published in 1936.

Anti-fascist pamphlet published in 1939.

According to Peter Adam in *Art of the Third Reich* (Harry N. Abrams, 1992): "The United States Government kept about 800 of the most inflammatory works in a vault under the auspices of the army in Washington." In 1946 the postwar German government in Bonn constitutionally banned Nazi symbology, especially the swastika, from any public display on penalty of a year imprisonment. In 1952 a second act banning all symbols by prohibited organizations was passed. In fact, in the 1960s, when the United States Army wanted to return hundreds of confiscated swastika-adorned artifacts it had seized to West Germany, Bonn refused to take possession (apparently the stash was dumped at sea). Yet this did not stifle use of the mark after the war. In a 1946 article titled "Nazi Symbols Used in 559 of 6,700 Entries in Contest for New German Postage Stamp," the *New York Times* reported that entrants in a nationwide competition to find postwar philately used the swastika overtly or "tried to inject subversive propaganda." By 1960, desecration of synagogues in Germany with swastikas was on the rise by individuals who were too young to remember the Nazi regime. Two twenty-five-year-old vandals in Cologne were sentenced to prison. In Stuttgart, a former West German Army soldier was given eleven months in prison for drawing swastikas on the blackboard in his barracks. A local court in Nuremberg sentenced a twenty-six-year-old to four months imprisonment for smearing swastikas on the walls of a railroad station. Police arrested Josef Schone, twenty-five years old, less than two months after he had gotten out of jail for the desecration of a synagogue. And Germany was not the only site of swastika revival: Three swastikas were cut into newly-laid concrete outside a cottage in Bristol, England, while in La Crosse, Wisconsin, two boys, eighteen and nineteen years old, were placed on two year's probation for painting swastikas on the walls of a synagogue. Also in 1960, the German state of Rhineland-Palatinate banned the extreme right-wing German Reichs party as an anticonstitutional neo-Nazi organization.

Cover of *Direction* magazine designed by Paul Rand, 1941.

The now-famous opening documentary sequence of the film Judgement at Nuremberg that showed a huge concrete swastika atop the Nuremberg stadium being dynamited to pieces marked the end of Nazi Germany, but the beginning of a continued cultist reverence for the symbol.

Legal prohibition has only strengthened the mythology and symbology of the swastika. Although its earlier mystic significance has been all but forgotten, its legacy as a Nazi emblem has increased in much the same way the occultists revered it as a measure of past

Jacket for *I Saw Hitler* by Dorothy Thompson, 1938.

glories. As the Nazi era passes further from living recollection into mythic memory, the danger exists that it will be revivified, not as a quaint mark of antiquity, but as a sign of false martyrdom for a(n) (un)holy cause.

chapter four

BENIGN DESIGN

If the symbol is used on an object or in connection with it, it may only be used if the object itself has an inner relation to the symbol [i.e., a badge or medal] … The use of symbols for publicity purposes is in any case forbidden.

—Joseph Goebbels, Law for Protection of National Symbols, May 19, 1933

Passaic's sample election ballots are covered with swastika emblems, but Fred Clough, the printer, hastened today to say that they were not the work of Chancellor Hitler. "I've used the swastika emblems for ballot borders long before the world ever knew Hitler," said Mr. Clough. "I have had the swastika emblems in my type chests for more than fifteen years."

—*The New York Times*, September 16, 1937

"Swastika, Canadian Town, Won't Yield Name to Hitler." This tiny northern Ontario town—population 261—was named long before Adolf Hitler adopted the Swastika as the symbol of Nazism, citizens decided at a meeting last night, said the town's name won't be changed.

—*Brooklyn Eagle* [AP], September 13, 1940

Cover of novelty pamphlet, 1930.

Despite its centrality in racist mysticism, between the late nineteenth and early twentieth centuries, the swastika was a largely benign emblem. Before its appropriation by Nazidom, the swastika was used innocently and frequently as a design motif on everything from architecture to consumables, signifying good fortune and well being. It was universally adopted by merchants and manufacturers on cigar labels and bands, fruit wrappers and box tops, business signs and logos, playing cards and poker chips. It even decorated something as mundane as a trivet, a cast iron holder on which hot irons were placed when not in use. As an architectural ornament, the swastika was frequently cast in stone or

Post cards with swastika as good luck symbol, c. 1920s.

masonry and is still extant on the cornices and moldings of old buildings. Similarly, it was sold as an interlocking border design for advertisements, made available through most prewar, hot-metal typeface catalogs for use on posters, calling cards, handbills, and book jackets. Author Rudyard Kipling combined a swastika with his signature in a circle as a personal logo on many early editions of his books, and also gave the name "Swastika" to editor Edward Bok's stately residence in Merion, Pennsylvania. However, in 1933, a few months after Hitler's rise to power, he ordered that the swastika not appear on his next book.

From the early teens through the mid-thirties, the swastika was as common a decorative device as the lozenge, leader dot, and sawtooth rule were in eighties and nineties postmodern graphic design. In 1910, the St. Louis, Rocky Mountain & Pacific Railway Company started using it as the centerpiece of the Rocky Mountain route logo. Coca-Cola issued a swastika good luck pendant during the teens. In the twenties the American Biscuit Company of San Francisco, California, prominently printed the swastika on the box of American Snow Flakes and American Soda Crackers. The United States Playing Card Company of Cincinnati, Ohio, registered it in 1921 as a trademark for "Fortune" playing cards. Carlsberg

Playing cards with swastika motif, c. 1920s.

Postcard with swastika good luck sign, c. 1920s.

Cigar bands and label, c. 1930s.

etched it onto the bottoms of their beer bottles until the mid-thirties. And the Boston Hose & Rubber Company of Cambridge, Massachusetts, included a counterclockwise version in the trademark of their "Good Luck Jar Rubbers." These are just a few of the countless American businesses that employed it simultaneously. Today as a commercial mark it would never be sanctioned by so many different companies lest it confuse brand-minded consumers. But back then, since no one held title to the mark—and it was so prevailingly understood—it was fair game for any company that wanted to evoke a goodwill image.

As benign design, prior to the 1933 Nazi prohibition of the swastika as a commercial mark, it was also the brand for scores of German manufacturers and industries, incorporated onto machines, posters, advertisements, and poster-stamps (miniature posters printed on stamps). German trademark design of this period was the most advanced of any Western industrialized country. Graphic designers, including Peter Beherens, Karl Schulpig, O.H.W. Haddank, Lucian Bernhard, Carlo Egler, Valetin Zietara, and Wilhelm Defke (who designed a swastika iteration that was used by the Nazis), introduced the reductive yet stark visual mark to the practice of business identity. Like the swastika itself,

GOOD✪LUCK
JAR RUBBERS

in the latest and most efficient shape
with the large handy single lip which
enables the jar to be opened instantly.
Made in the famous GOOD LUCK
quality known to canning experts
and housewives everywhere.

Advertisement for Good Luck Jar
Rubbers, 1929.

TOP: Label for fireworks package, c. 1946.

CENTER: Lable for matchbox, c. 1950s.

BOTTOM: Original Bauhaus logo, 1919.

these marks—both abstract and representational—were quintessentially memorable. As a symbol of the sun, suggesting rebirth, it was extolled by artist Paul Klee and included in the very first logo of the Bauhaus, the state design school where he was a master instructor. It was removed from subsequent iterations that were designed in the manner of the "new typography," which was ultimately repudiated by the Nazis because it was a rejection of völkisch Fraktur lettering. And despite the Bauhaus' former links to the swastika—and its contribution to efficient information design—the Nazis closed down the school for being seditiously avant garde.

Elsewhere in Europe the swastika was a common piece of decorative iconography. In Hungary, for example, where decorated eggs are popular in folk art, the swastika was frequently painted on as a sun wheel—each arm represented a base element: water, earth, air, and fire. On some eggs, a spinning swastika symbol was called a "crab tail."

During World War I, an orange swastika on a red field was the shoulder patch of the American 45th Infantry Division, until 1939 when it was changed to a thunderbird. Originally, the four "legs" of the swastika represented the four states that the 45th comprised: Arizona, Colorado, New Mexico, and Utah (it is also said

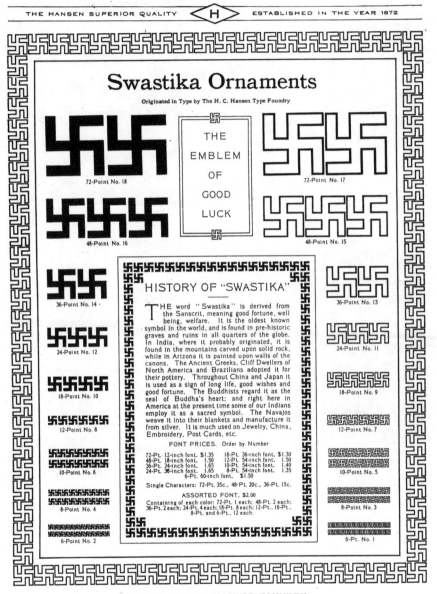

Swastika Ornaments

Originated in Type by The H. C. Hansen Type Foundry

72-Point No. 18

THE
EMBLEM
OF
GOOD
LUCK

72-Point No. 17

48-Point No. 16

48-Point No. 15

36-Point No. 14

36-Point No. 13

24-Point No. 12

24-Point No. 11

18-Point No. 10

18-Point No. 9

12-Point No. 8

12-Point No. 7

10-Point No. 6

10-Point No. 5

8-Point No. 4

8-Point No. 3

6-Point No. 2

6-Pt. No. 1

HISTORY OF "SWASTIKA"

THE word "Swastika" is derived from the Sanscrit, meaning good fortune, well being, welfare. It is the oldest known symbol in the world, and is found in pre-historic graves and ruins in all quarters of the globe. In India, where it probably originated, it is found in the mountains carved upon solid rock, while in Arizona it is painted upon walls of the canons. The Ancient Greeks, Cliff Dwellers of North America and Brazilians adopted it for their pottery. Throughout China and Japan it is used as a sign of long life, good wishes and good fortune. The Buddhists regard it as the seal of Buddha's heart; and right here in America at the present time some of our Indians employ it as a sacred symbol. The Navajos weave it into their blankets and manufacture it from silver. It is much used on Jewelry, China, Embroidery, Post Cards, etc.

FONT PRICES. Order by Number

72-Pt.	12-inch font,	$1.35	18-Pt. 36-inch font,	$1.30
48-Pt.	18-inch font,	1.50	12-Pt. 54-inch font,	1.50
36-Pt.	24-inch font,	1.65	10-Pt. 54-inch font,	1.40
24-Pt.	36-inch font,	1.65	8-Pt. 54-inch font,	1.35
	6-Pt. 60-inch font,	$1.50		

Single Characters: 72-Pt. 35c., 48-Pt. 20c., 36-Pt. 15c.

ASSORTED FONT, $2.00

Containing of each color: 72-Pt. 1 each; 48-Pt. 2 each; 36-Pt. 2 each; 24-Pt. 4 each; 18-Pt. 8 each; 12-Pt., 10-Pt., 8-Pt. and 6-Pt., 12 each.

THE H. C. HANSEN TYPE FOUNDRY

Type specimen page for H. C. Hansen Type Foundry catalog, 1928.

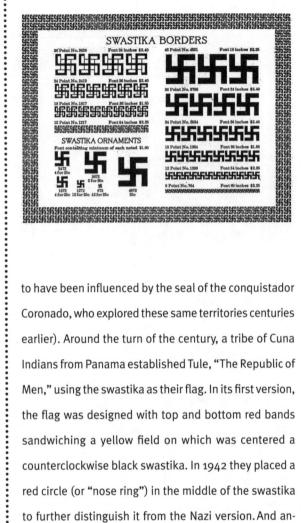

TOP RIGHT: Swastika borders from Barnhart Brothers type catalog, 1924.

TOP: Trivet with swastika, c. 1920s.

BOTTOM: Logo for Fortune playing cards, 1924.

to have been influenced by the seal of the conquistador Coronado, who explored these same territories centuries earlier). Around the turn of the century, a tribe of Cuna Indians from Panama established Tule, "The Republic of Men," using the swastika as their flag. In its first version, the flag was designed with top and bottom red bands sandwiching a yellow field on which was centered a counterclockwise black swastika. In 1942 they placed a red circle (or "nose ring") in the middle of the swastika to further distinguish it from the Nazi version. And another official emblem, a light blue swastika or Haka Risti, remained the marking on Finland's air force planes until 1945, even though they were not allies of Germany.

Consistent with the fashion for the swastika in late nineteenth and early twentieth-century Europe,

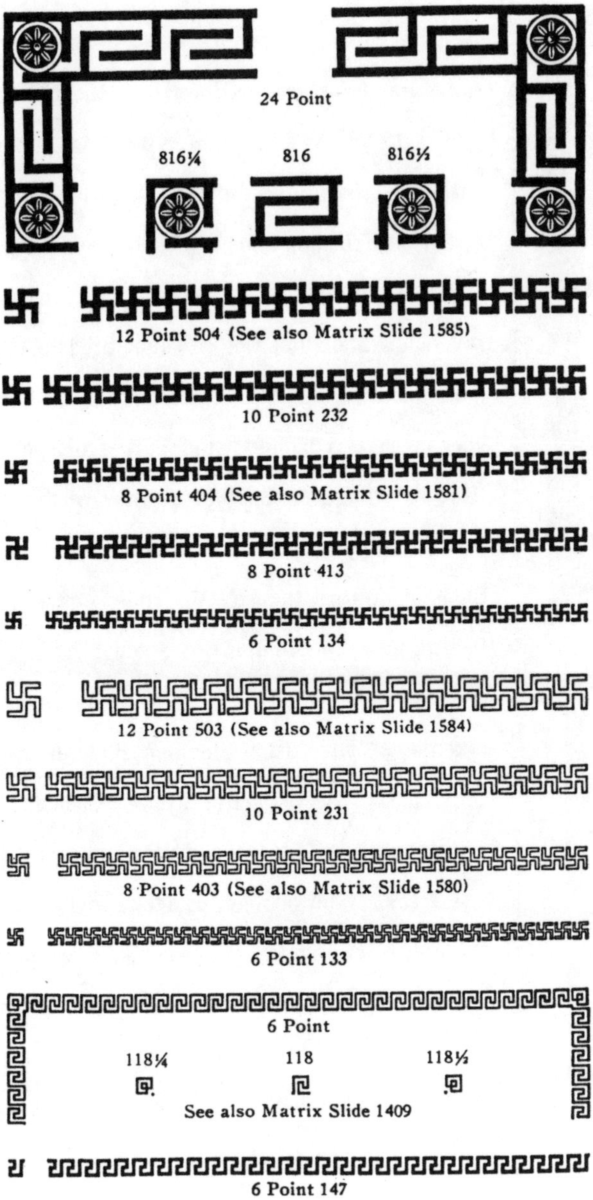

24 Point

816¼   816   816½

12 Point 504 (See also Matrix Slide 1585)

10 Point 232

8 Point 404 (See also Matrix Slide 1581)

8 Point 413

6 Point 134

12 Point 503 (See also Matrix Slide 1584)

10 Point 231

8 Point 403 (See also Matrix Slide 1580)

6 Point 133

6 Point

118¼   118   118½

See also Matrix Slide 1409

6 Point 147

Decorative borders from type catalog, c. 1920s.

TOP: Ex Libris for L. F. Salzmann, 1899.

CENTER: Binding with Rudyard Kipling's personal logo, 1912.

BOTTOM: Cover for *Tanglewood Tales* with meandering swastika design, c. 1915.

swastika clubs representing various social or professional groups were formed throughout the United States as well. None was as popular as the Girls' Club, whose nationally-distributed monthly magazine (published by Curtis Publishing Company in Philadelphia between 1914 and 1918) was called *The Swastika*. Each issue had cover illustration that routinely integrated the swastika motif into a cartoon-like vignette. The club's treasured keepsake was a diamond studded swastika pin, advertised as "What Every Girl Wants — Her Own Swastika."

The Boy Scouts were also the beneficiaries of the mark. In 1910, the Excelsior Shoe Company, manufacturers of the Original Boy Scout Shoe, used the swastika as a logo and issued a swastika-emblazoned token as an advertising premium. Baden-Powell, the venerable founder of the Boy Scouts, explained in *What Scouts Can Do: More Yarns* in 1921 that he developed a "Swastika Thanks Badge" as a token of brotherhood: "Whatever its origin... the Swastika now stands for the Badge of Fellowship among Scouts all over the world," he wrote, "and when anyone has done a kindness to a Scout it is their privilege to present him — or her — with this token of their gratitude, which makes

90

Spoon with swastika ornament, c. 1910.

TOP: Illustration from magic catalog, 1925.

BOTTOM: Label for deodorant cream, c. 1920s.

91

ABOVE: Cover for *The Swastika* magazine, 1913.

OPPOSITE: Covers of *The Swastika*, 1914–16.

CLOCKWISE FROM TOP LEFT:
Cover from Girls Club brochure with swastika emblem, 1913.

Cover of *The Swastika*, 1915.

How to earn the Girls Club swastika emblem, 1913.

Cover of *The Swastika*, 1916.

The Girls Club emblem booklet, 1913.

Girls Club flyer, 1914.

him a sort of member of the Brotherhood and entitles him to the help of any other Scout at any time and at any place." In this spirit, the Boy Scouts established an "Order of the White Swastika" in Portsmouth, Ohio, Camp Russell, New York, and St. Joseph, Missouri. Over the course of twelve weekends, scouts competed in twelve different skills. Boys who fulfilled their tasks received a white swastika badge. By 1940, however, the symbol was beginning to tarnish. At the Boy Scout jamboree in Santiago, Chile, Boy and Girl Scout leaders abandoned the swastika. They had used it as a symbol of distinguished service for thirty-one years, but Scout officers wearing medals with the insignia had become the object of criticism and protest when parading the streets.

As a lucky charm, or lucky cross as it was also known, the swastika appears as the focal point in a book for children entitled *Bing-o*, about a mischievous little monkey who is given a magic charm with a swastika. The text reads: "'As long as you wear it . . . everything will be easy,' says a wise old owl." During the late twenties, a classical music ensemble, the Swastika Quartet, gave a concert at Town Hall, and while their name suggested good fortune, the critics found that the quality of some of their playing was unfortunate. Luck played a role in why the Swastika Hotel, built in 1929 in Raton, New

Poker chips, c. 1920s.

VOL. IV — No. 9

September — 1913

The Swastika

Written and Read by The Girls' Club

ANNIVERSARY NUMBER

Cover for *The Swastika* magazine, 1913.

Cover (above) and inside page (opposite) from *Bing-o*,
by Tom Lamb, c. 1932.

Advertising trade stamps,
c. 1920s.

Mexico, was given the name, although it was changed to the Yucca Hotel during World War II. And in Iowa, first among corn producers, the famous Corn Palace was decorated with thousands of ears of corn arranged in the sign of the swastika. One might say they were lucky that the building did not burn to the ground given the combustibility of the decorative material.

Following the Nazi's defeat, the swastika was utterly reviled, but in the United States, it was also used increasingly on paperback book covers for spy and mystery yarns and on covers of pulp men's adventure magazines. Even today, the most common, sanctioned mainstream use of the mark is on jackets for fiction and nonfiction books with World War II themes. In the late forties and fifties, the male public's fascination with things Nazi was disturbingly fetishistic, and to an extent it still is. Yet publishers knew what they were doing from a marketing standpoint; the swastika was such an identifiable icon—a magnet, so to speak—that a browser could perceive content without ever reading the title. It is indeed ironic that the swastika has evolved from benevolent sign to sinister national emblem to veritable point-of-purchase display in only a few generations. The latter's only virtue is that it continues to represent the unspeakable crimes of Hitler's Germany.

Swastika brand fruit label,
c. 1930s.

However, as these critical events fade into the past, each time the swastika is aestheticized on a book jacket or a movie poster, its rhetorical strength diminishes, to the ultimate detriment of its historical significance.

Advertising trade stamp,
c. 1920s.

ABOVE: Sheet music cover for "Swastika Valse," c. 1912.

OPPOSITE, TOP: Finnish airforce fighter (F2A-1 buffalo) with blue against white swastika marking, 1939.

OPPOSITE, CENTER: Shoulder patch for the U.S. Army, 1918.

OPPOSITE, BOTTOM: Postcard of the Iowa Corn Palace, c. 1930.

TOP: Native American blanket/scarf, c. 1930s.

CENTER: Boy Scout good luck tokens, 1930s.

BOTTOM: Cloisonné swastika pin, 1932.

Cover of the *World of Men*, 1956.

chapter five

HITLER'S CHILDREN

New Delhi. The formation of an Indian Nazi party with the swastika as its symbol and dictatorship as its aim was announced today. The party promised that if its suggestions were followed, within 20 years India would be "the strongest power on this planet."

—*The New York Times*, June 29, 1967

For the better part of the twentieth century, the emblems and icons of communism were inviolable; desecration was a criminal offense. Then, overnight, they were removed and destroyed as if infected by some disease. With the surprise breakup of the Soviet Union in 1991, the hammer and sickle, the bulwark of Bolshevik revolution and symbol of Communist rule, was replaced throughout the Iron Curtain by flags and coats of arms dating back to pre-Communist monarchies. Venerable symbols provided a strong, if archaic, alternative to the symbols of totalitarianism. Although some of these old trappings were as abhorrent in their day as the hammer and sickle was, for a generation born under the Red Star

Poster for Russian Fascist organization, 1991.

it was better to identify with the vagary of old nationalism than the reality of decayed communism.

Many former Warsaw Pact nations replaced communism with nationalism. Those who were starved for freedom found succor in the bosom of patriotism and, therefore, embraced nostalgia for a bygone era before most were born. The refuge of nationalism, which philosopher Erich Fromm described as a form of incest, became a convenient way to channel decades of seething resentment. Nationalism allowed those who were subjugated by the state to redirect their pent-up passions toward renewal. But nationalism is not a cure-all. As André Gide warned: "The nationalist has a broad hatred and a narrow love." The poet Paul Valéry added that "All nations have present, or past, or future reasons for thinking themselves incomparable."

In the early 1990s, to fuel the flames of rebellion and, once achieved, fill the vacuum left by an all-controlling ideology, nationalism quickly spread throughout the former communist world. As the nations of the communist bloc were freed from occupation and domination, the symptoms of nationalism described by Gide emerged. The breakup of the Soviet republics, the partition of Czechoslovakia, the dissolution of Yugoslavia, and the reunification of Germany are evidence that communism had only temporarily mooted the tribal/nation-alistic prejudices that had fomented below the surface since World War II. Owing to communism's draconian squelching of ethnic and religious strife, nationalism was revisited with indescribable fervor. And ironically, after almost half a century, the same rhetoric that had underscored Nazism in the early 1930s—extreme nation-alism—reemerged with a vengeance in the 1990s.

In this spirit the swastika, and the emblems inspired by it, were revived and reused by nationalist groups in many former Communist countries. In some they were even given official legitimacy. Where the dis-mantling of Communist apparatus left chaos (or where former Communist snakes have shed their old skin for new), the promise of a "new order" (a term synonymous with fascism) had great appeal. The frightening resur-gence of Nazi-inspired symbols and regalia in Russia, Germany, and Eastern Europe rose despite their nega-tive historical connotations. That most of the groups, movements, and paramilitary militias that adopted these images were on the radical political fringe did not relegate them to the margins. Like the Nazis before them, they fomented disruption as a means to achieve power within the mainstream. Indeed some of the eth-nic and religious prejudice that underscores many of

Eastern Europe's and the former Soviet Union's armed conflicts today are fought under neo-fascist banners.

The Soviet Union, and Czarist Russia before it, was riddled with anti-Semitism; similarly in the early 1990s, there emerged a virulent strain among ultra–right-wing groups calling for old-fashioned pogroms and new-tyled ethnic cleansing. While nestled on the fringe, this decidedly organized melange of monarchist, neo-fascist, and Pamyat (or "memory") organizations openly hawked their ideologies on the street, until Boris Yeltsin's October 1993 emergency decrees banned opposition media. Polemical newspapers with the titles *Russia Arise*, *The Russian New Order*, and *People's Business*, featuring realistic drawings of heroic-looking black-shirted Russian storm troopers, scabrous anti-Semitic caricatures, and portraits of Adolf Hitler himself were unashamedly displayed at sidewalk tables throughout Moscow and St. Petersburg. Various iterations of the swastika, sometimes combined with historic Russian folk iconography, were also in full view. A visitor to Moscow reported that it was impossible to walk a block without running into at least one of these displays.

While the long-term political objectives of Russian fascist groups were confused, their immediate mission was stated in their literature: "massing forces and train-

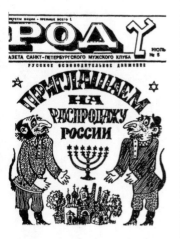

Cover of *Family*, an anti-Semitic nationalist newspaper, 1991.

ing our bodies for when the power comes." Given the economic instability in current Russia, these forces are potentially as potent as when the Soviet Union fell. Today, one of the largest yet most factionalized right-wing organization is the Pamyat, which is dedicated to recalling a past that had been expunged by the Communists. In fact, they have reclaimed the double-headed Czarist eagle as their national symbol. While some of Pamyat's factions, reminded of the bloody toll exacted on Russians in World War II, deny fascist leanings, others are visibly tied to the Nazis through their regalia—black shirt, leather shoulder strap and belt, combat boots, and swastika armband. The Pamyat swastika combines an ancient Russian design with the hooked cross, similar to that used by World War II–era Russian fascists, who grew in number during the 1938 Nazi-Soviet Pact, but were purged by Stalin after the Nazi invasion. Current members are former youth gang members known as the lyubery (named for a dangerous low-rent suburb of Moscow), whose mission is, in the words of one of its members, "ridding Russia of the Jews, the Chechens, the Georgians, the Tartars, the Armenians and the other black asses..." In a 1993 interview in the *Moscow Guardian*, a member admitted: "I became a fascist to help revive Great Russia. It's been turned into an American colony by the Yids and the Masons. We'd never have allowed the Americans to meddle in our lives—and we'll make the Yankee go home!"

The most militant of these factions adopted many of the Nazi slogans and icons. "He who puts on a black shirt today pledges allegiance to the homeland and the nation with the words Russia or Death," wrote an anonymous Pamyat member in "About Russian Nationalism or Why We Wear Black Shirts," an essay in a 1992 pamphlet called The Russian Era. In their appropriation of the black shirt (originally adopted in 1922 as the uniform of the Italian Fascists) and the red, white, and black swastika armband, they recalled the 1930s, when shirt colors delineated fascist groups in Germany (brown), Ireland (blue), and America (gold). They further returned to the period when graphic emblems were as powerful as weapons and variations of the blood-and-iron symbols, such as the Italian faces and Nazi swastika, were adopted in Rumania (the iron cross), Croatia (the U for Ustasa), France (the cross of Lorraine), and even Switzerland (a Nazified variation of the Swiss cross).

Russian "liberation movements" dot the body politic. Some factions revived czarist and pre-czarist symbols; others combine the Nazi swastika with the Russian Orthodox cross. The St. Petersburg Men's Club,

The symbol of a Russian Fascist organization using Russian iconography and swastika, 1991.

Cover of *Pamyat*, a Russian nationalist newspaper, 1991.

Illustration from *Family*, combining Jewish star with swastika, 1919.

which published a newspaper called *People's Business*, used the imperial double-headed eagle, in which was inset a hooked cross resembling a Nautilus scepter. The Russian National Unity organization, which published an anti-Semitic newspaper titled Family (referring to the family of Russia), continues to use a twisted variation of the letter Y, akin to a runic letter.

Before Yeltsin's emergency decrees, fascists freely wore their uniforms on the streets, while in the basements of their headquarters they practiced the Nazi salute, martial arts, target practice, and engaged in other "Teutonic" rituals. However, once the restrictive decrees were in place, the most "moderate" leader of Pamyat threw his support behind Yeltsin against the hard-line Communists. But the hard-line militants went further underground. Given Russian democracy's fragility, bans against dangerous opponents continue; nonetheless the fanatical opposition pursue policies of destabilization, waiting for a total collapse of reforms.

Russia is not alone in the apparent trend towards fascist resurgence. Since its reunification Germany has been the scene of neo-Nazi violence against foreigners (mostly Turkish immigrants, but also others from Eastern Bloc countries who had fled before the fall of the Soviet Union). During the mid-1990s an infestation of skinheads, typically disaffected working class men and boys primarily from the former East Germany, terrorized the nation in daily skirmishes and assaults on civilians and police. These acts are not unlike those of their brown-shirted forebears in the early days of the Nazi party and are supported by organized neo-Nazi elders. Though the German government has successfully controlled the rate of incidents in recent years, they have not rid the country of its underground groups. Before reunification, armed right-wing paramilitary groups posing as sports and hunting clubs existed in Germany in defiance of federal law. The leaders of the new generation of storm troopers come from these older, organized, outlawed political groups. During the mid-1990s, the American Ku Klux Klan publicly offered to German fascists "advisors" in the "art" of street brawling. Although German stability is strong, like their Russian counterparts the German fascists have been preparing themselves for the cataclysm that will destabilize the government.

Most Germans are quick to disavow any return to fascism, and the constitutional law outlawing the swastika is but one instrument in the constant vigil. Nonetheless organized fascist groups persevered by adopting new symbols and regalia. Black shirts were replaced by light blue or gray ones, worn over black

Symbols of German neo-Nazi organizations that use swastika-derived and runic elements, 1993.

Symbol of the National Front, c. 1989.

pants. The Nationalist Front, a leader among the right-wing paramilitary associations, continues to march under the imperial flag; they also wear a shoulder patch with a runic symbol that looks more like the AIDS ribbon than a swastika. A diamond with feet called an Odalrune, which was used by a Nazi-era SS battalion, is also the mark of the right-wing Bundes Nationaler Sudenten (BNS), a neo-fascist organization based on the model of the Hitler Youth. Other outlawed groups that invoke symbolic echoes of Nazi Germany are Volkssozialis-tischen Bewegung Deutschlands/Partei der Arbeit, whose symbol resembles a printer's register mark or gun sight; the Aktionsfront Nationaler Sozialsten/Nati-noaler Aktivisten, and the Jungen Front, both of which have symbols that resemble the lightning bolt or "S" used by the SS.

Despite the government ban on public demonstra-tions, proliferation of such groups, such as The National-ist Front, The Deutsche Alternativ, and The New Front, continues. In 1992 together they were blamed for over 1,800 criminal acts against foreigners. But in recent years heavy surveillance has been maintained by Germany's Federal Office for Protection of the Constitution. And former German Chancellor Helmut Kohl announced in 1995: "Whoever thinks that they can change our land with a climate of intimidation and fear, they are fooling themselves." Nonetheless, according to officials, before The Deutscher Alternativ party was banned, it had gained considerable power at the local level, particularly in eastern German towns near the Polish border, where widespread unemployment has been exacerbated by the illegal entry of foreigners.

Because neo-Nazis are prohibited from exhibiting inflammatory iconography, the propagation of their faith often comes through music, which is protected under the constitution. The driving, pounding rhythms of German hate rock songs have moved fans of neo-Nazi rock, known as "Oi musik," into the streets. A song by the band called Böhse Onkelz (Evil Uncles) reached number five on the German pop charts. Störkraft (Destructive Force), a Düsseldorf-based skinhead band, made television appearances, although not singing lyrics that advocate violence against Turks and others. According to the *New York Times*: "Oi music's allure appears strongest in formerly Communist lands of East Europe, where the economic and social structures that young people grew up with collapsed almost overnight..." The *Times* also reported that some East European bands actually make the German groups seem moderate. In Hungary, a former Communist country that on the surface does not seem to have been hit with as much transitional turmoil as Yugoslavia, a band called Cigany Puszitito Garda (Gypsy Destroyers Guard Regiment) openly display Hungary's fascist emblem from World War II and play to packed houses with songs like "Gypsy-Free Zone," featuring lyrics like:

> The flame-thrower is the only weapon
> With which I can triumph
> Exterminate the Gypsies
> Whether child, woman, or man

During the initial partition of Yugoslavia during the early 1990s, the Croatian fascist paramilitary known as Ustasa (Stand Up, as in for the cause) was neither underground nor alternative. They were sanctioned paramilitary combatants. Ustasa was the black-shirted Croatian fascist party from World War II whose leader, Dr. Ante Pavelic, ran the puppet state for the Nazis. Since the breakup in 1992 of Yugoslavia and the recognition of Croatia (first by Bonn) as an independent nation, the U symbolizing the Ustasa has also reemerged as an official emblem for military irregulars. Photographic stickers of Pavelic's official portrait have also appeared "unofficially" pasted on official vehicles and weapons.

Members of the Afrikaner Resistance Movement (AWB) after seige of
Johannesburg World Trade Center, 1993.

In addition swastikas, which were never outlawed in Yugoslavia, have appeared on walls in combat areas and on uniforms of paramilitary combatants. In Zagreb the Croatian capital's black-shirted auxiliary police help patrol the city's streets and occupy a building (which, with the approval of the government, they commandeered from the society of graphic artists) in the center of the town. While the Croatian government has not openly embraced fascism, it has tolerated the presence of this fascist organization.

The resurgence of fascism in the former Communist countries is not simply the predictable response to years of deep-seated disaffection, but of a greater social malady—ignorance. For the Nazi-inspired emblems and icons being revived and displayed in public strongly suggest that the new fascist acolytes accept the tenets of an ideology that embraced racism and genocide as viable policy instruments. Members of these organizations, many of whom do not have a first-hand experience with the fascist past, flaunt their contraband symbols in Germany and Russia under the watchful eyes of the authorities, while those in Croatia proudly display them without threat of prosecution. In both cases the goal is to use symbols that are still virulent as a means to shock and intimidate.

Leader of the banned AWB in
Brussels, c. 1993.

Wherever Nazi-inspired symbols are found—the
black shirt, swastika, and other hooked cross variations—violence appears to be inevitable. In June 1993
armed members of the South African Afrikaner Resistance Movement (AWB), wearing a swastika-inspired
emblem composed of three 7s in a circle surrounded
by a red field, stormed their way into the Johannesburg
World Trade Center, where negotiations concerning the
end of white-dominated rule were in progress. Today
ultra-right apartheid groups have been forced underground, but the organizations for which these symbols
stand remain a threat.

T-shirt design of Aryan symbol with Nazi-era swastika, 1989.

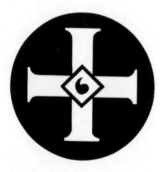

Symbol of the Ku Klux Klan.

Although neutral during World War II, Switzerland also had a fascist party. The Federation Fasciste Suisse was allied with the Italian Fascists during the war and continue to this day. Their symbol, a nazified variation of the national Swiss cross, is currently used by the neo-Nazi Front Patriotique, an organization with ties to so-called "national fronts" in England, France, and Belgium.

American fascist groups have maintained a long history. The German/American Bund boasted 3 million members before being banned in 1941. Neo-Nazis came out from under the sheets long ago, when in the 1950s George Lincoln Rockwell led a small American Nazi party. White supremacy groups routinely march in public, free from the threat of prosecution. Racist and hate groups use evocative emblems to both distinguish between themselves and signify their goals. The Ku Klux Klan uses a cross on which a symbolic drop of blood is inset, suggesting its appeal to martyrdom, brotherhood, and terror. WAR (White Aryan Resistance) of Fallbrook, California, uses a skull and crossbones with an eye patch (a perversely comic Jolly-Roger version of the SS death's head) on a heraldic shield, indicating the guerrilla nature of this group, whose skinheads are trained in urban violence. The Aryan Nations' emblem carves through an expanded N with a sword, on which sits a crown set on a heraldic shield that emits the rays of power, suggesting decidedly distorted religious roots (not unlike the Nazi "NSV" symbol). The American Front weds a gun sight with its initials; though awkwardly designed, it indicates their preferred means of redress.

The propagation of American fascism comes in many forms. WAR publishes a newspaper that advertises "Racist Video Tapes," "Suggested Reading for Aryans," and "Blood and Honour Merchandise." The items offered in the latter are the usual swastika patches and pins, but also include an ironic emblem: One of the swastikas in this package is appropriated from John Heartfield's famous anti-Nazi collage published in the *AIZ* (1939), "The Old Motto In The 'New Reich:' Blood and Iron," showing four axes forming a swastika. In its day it was a stinging indictment of a bloodthirsty regime, yet today, co-opted by the radical right, it is a badge of honor.

The Internet has become a major outlet for the dissemination of hate materials to a much larger number of would-be initiates. The sites are easy to access, and for those who find allure in the trappings of Nazidom, there is no mistaking the graphics—spiky black-letter typefaces and swastika-inspired logos. The site for Stormfront, a right-wing skinhead group, displays the

Symbol of the White Aryan Resistance, c. 1980.

Symbol of the American Front, c. 1980.

White Power bumper sticker for the
National Socialist White People's
Party, c. 1978.

Großdeutschland eagle and SS runic logo (for the NS
88 Video Division). The National Alliance home page
graphics, on the other hand, are decidedly more benign,
and therefore more deceptive. The three-dimensional
forked-cross logo (reminiscent of an elongated peace
symbol), framed by laurel leaves and set against a blue
sky, looks like any network television graphic. The uniform headline typeface and overall composition of the
National Alliance home page is comparable to any pro-
fessionally-produced site. Meanwhile, The Underground
Resistance (The Resistance Records Home Page) uses
another strong mainstream-inspired design. A melange
of computer-enhanced, shining typefaces and hot buttons to access information screens and music selections
(for such groups as Rahowa's, short for "racial holy war")
are produced in full color. Photos of the record covers
and group members are more stylishly professional than
typical hate material. Even the typography for Aryan

Nations' home page utilizes a hip digital typeface found on youth sites all over the Internet.

The most updated variation of the swastika has emerged on the Internet in the form of the "Reichstar," the symbol of the neo-Nazi group called Reichsfolk, which appears on their newsletter, Western Avatar. "Its purpose is not to replace the swastika," claims the group, "and Reichsfolk fully honours the swastika as the

Illegal meeting of neo-Nazi group in Germany, c. 1990.

Earth-bound symbol of the Third Reich, its heroes and martyrs, and the continuing struggle of the National-Socialist Cause..." The Reichstar, comprised of four unconnected hooks with razor-sharp–looking ends in a circle, is designed to be displayed at Reichsfolk gatherings "as a banner/flag—and upon all those attending, as an arm-band, pendant or ring."

Throughout the 1990s Nazi iconography has held a dangerous fascination for those who hold the racist beliefs espoused by Hitler. For a generation far removed from the horrors he wrought, his signs and symbols rekindle atavistic tribal hatreds. Fifty years after the fall of the Third Reich, the flame of ignorance is kept burning in large degree by the continued currency of the swastika.

chapter six

HEIL, HEIL,
ROCK 'N' ROLL

The roots of their rebellion lie in the trappings of an old mystique—and in a newer one, of swastikas and iron crosses and cast-off overcoats and garish hearses whose original meaning have long since broken and washed away, where only the spirit remains, to haunt the beachboys of Waikiki.

—William Cleary, *Surfing: All the Young Wave Hunters*, 1967

A punk asked by Time Out... why she wore a swastika, replied: 'Punks just like to be hated.'

—Dick Hebdige, *Subculture: The Meaning of Style*, 1979

A problem that has long plagued downtown Washington, the deface-ment of newspaper boxes and trash bins by spray painted swastikas and SS logos, appears to be spreading into residential communities...

—*The New York Times*, April 12, 1996

Logo for ZZ Flex skateboards, c. 1990.

A cultural literacy exam given to selected New York City high school students, within months after the release of Stephen Spielberg's movie, *Schindler's List*, revealed that over 30 percent of those tested could not place the Holocaust—the genocidal murder of 6 million Jews and millions of others—in a proper historical context. As this cataclysmic event further fades in time, there is a very real threat that kids will become ignorant of Nazi crimes.

The evidence of such ignorance takes many insidious forms, including the increasingly popular and flagrant abuse and reapplication of Nazi-inspired iconography as logos for products like skateboards and CD albums. Infusing very dangerous symbols with romance not only steals historical relevance from heinous imagery, but reduces its cautionary power. The young, who are not as well versed in this vocabulary, are thereby desensitized to the political red flags around them.

In Germany, a constitutional law prohibits the public display of the swastika and other Nazi symbols of any kind, punishable by harsh penalties. In America, no such law exists. Nor should there be, given the doctrine of free speech. This license, however, does not mean that these venal icons can be used on commercial whim. Their meaning is as unambiguous as the Final Solution. Not just the swastika, but other Nazi graphic emblems represent the ideology of a barbarous regime. Today, fifty years after the Third Reich was defeated, Nazi-inspired images have become benign clip art to be decoupaged on skateboards, fashion labels, and CD covers. In an age where sampling and biting corporate and brand logos is an expression of political frustration, some graphic artist/designers contend that stealing Nazi images is also a polemical act. Reclaiming or co-opting the swastika neutralizes, satirizes, or demystifies these images, they claim. These are the smart ones. The less astute find Nazi imagery, well, "just kinda cool." Sometimes it's difficult to know which group is the most ignorant: the ones who strive for the intellectual high ground or the ones who are clueless. And while most view the symbols mindlessly, all you have to do is surf the Internet to find those marks emblazoned on a score of home pages for white supremacists, skin heads, and hatemongers.

Granted, popular art has been eroding the historical memory of the symbol since the 1950s, when men's magazines reduced black-shirted Nazis to villainous Simon Legrees. "In the popular culture of the West, Nazism was often no more than a source of light-hearted amusement, of distraction, perverse fascination and even sadomasochistic pornography," writes Robert S. Wistrich, in *Weekend in Munich: Art Propaganda and Terror in The Third Reich* (Trafalgar Square, 1996). During the 1960s California surf culture adopted Nazi symbolism as means of displaying antiestablishment rebellion. Ironically, the symbol was first used in this context in advertisements for the 1930 Swastika Surfboard Company ("Ride the Swastika"), yet thirty years later the term "surf nazi" was popularized to describe this apolitical subculture which wore German military apparel and swastika medals. Clearly, any moral and political lessons to be drawn from Nazi terror and genocide are bound to be dulled by such mischievous and irresponsible approaches to the past. The reduction of Nazism to nothing

CD for Sacred Reich, c. 1993.

more than the object of fun is an example, concludes Wistrich, of the politics of forgetting.

More recent memory loss can be traced back to 1973, when Kiss began playing heavy metal music and wearing fright makeup. Their logo, inspired by comic book lettering in a gothic style, became the standard for heavy metal graphic design. It also marked the first time since the end of the Third Reich that Nazi iconography was re-aestheticized for mainstream consumption. The last two letters of the band's name, SS, are virtually identical to the insignia of the Schutzstaffel (SS), Hitler's elite branch of the Nazi military/police that administered the Final Solution. Though few critics questioned the reference, there was no mistaking it for the nazified lightning bolts, known as "SS runes," a letter that type founders were required to include in the official German alphabet during the Third Reich.

A Kiss fan denied the association in a letter to the *AIGA Journal of Graphic Design* (Vol 14, No. 2), saying: "The stylized SS in the logo were never intended, nor do they have anything whatsoever to do with, the Schutzstaffel. The logo was created by the original guitarist, Paul Ace Frehley, who has said time and again that the Nazi reference was never intended."

In any case, intent is not the issue; history is. Un-

LEFT: Logo for the D.C. United soccer team (USA), 1997.

RIGHT: Großdeutschland eagle on logo for the Deutsche Reichsbahn, 1936.

less the "SS" insignia is forever consigned to the cabinet of inviolable icons, the mark should remain a symbol of evil. Its history is robbed, its symbolism sanitized, when it is flagrantly displayed as an accouterment of rock performance. Whether they knew it or not (and since three of the original Kiss members are Jewish, ignorance probably prevails over malicious intent), Kiss's adaptation of this image, which was printed on twelve albums, a score of T-shirts and other souvenirs, and spawned countless imitators, is an insult to the victims and survivors of Nazi terror.

The graphics of the Nazi party have been referred to as the most effective identity system in history. The swastika was integrated into hundreds of official logos, emblems, and insignia and inspired countless unofficial versions that were also popular political and commercial graphic devices. Today, collector's catalogs of Nazi-era imagery, including equally-charged ancillary icons, are widely available and used by contemporary designers as a resource.

Of the growing litany of depoliticized Nazi forms, the Boy London logo is a vivid example of historical amnesia and flagrant misappropriation. The motto for this fashion manufacturer and retailer is: "The strength of the country lies in its youth." Its trademark is nothing

Logo for Boy London, a clothing store, 1996.

less than the seal of Großdeutschland, or greater Germany, the official emblem of the Third Reich. The original version is an eagle with outstretched wings, its talons firmly embedded in a circle containing the swastika. Boy London's adaptation has the eagle sitting atop the O in the word boy.

Although the swastika is eliminated, the appropriation of such an historically charged image begs inquiry into the designer's motives. It is doubtful that this particular retailer, who markets to a gay clientele, wants to be associated with the Nazis. Yet when posed with the problem of designing a logo, the designer must have felt the seal of Großdeutschland made tremendous formal sense. It is imposing, memorable, and for godsakes, an eagle. When used on Boy London's expensive metal-covered diary and address book, they look like the official papers the Nazis were so fond of issuing.

Another example of reused Nazi imagery was found in supermarket butcher departments throughout the American South and West in 1988. As reported in *Time* and *Newsweek*, The Fleming Food Companies, an Oklahoma City–based food wholesaler, distributed promotional posters that resembled a forgotten Nazi-era image originally designed in 1936 by Ludwig Holhwein to

136

promote the Hitler Youth. The Fleming version, designed by the ad agency Sully & Wood, is a painting of a cowboy wearing chaps in an heroic pose tightly holding an American flag, above which a headline reads "America's Meat Roundup." Its Nazi roots went unnoticed until a college student was reminded of an illustration of a recruitment poster in his history textbook titled "Der Deutsche Student." A company spokesperson insisted at the time that the Fleming artist had worked from a live model, but the resemblance to Holhwein's Aryan superboy was indisputable.

Although Ludwig Holhwein is a renowned poster artist, some of his best work was done for the Nazi party. Does the fact that he was a master of poster art mitigate the heinous acts for which his posters now stand? Can the lessons of that era be so distant from reality that form can be separated from content? Nazi propaganda was extremely efficient, but should contemporary designers be able to sample at will, and desecrate the memory of the twentieth century's most bloodthirsty period, by separating good design from bad Germans? Design responsibility does not end with refusing to design for bad clients, but in refusing to design with bad images that have indelible connotations.

A designer who preferred to remain anonymous,

Poster for America's Meat Roundup, 1989.

Poster for Der Deutsche Student, designed by Ludwig Hohlwein in 1938.

quoted in the *AIGA Journal of Graphic Design*, Vol 14, No. 1), talked about the logo of his New York band: "I've never used the swastika directly in my work, but I have twisted it around and distorted it while keeping the strong graphic look... While I don't want [my] band to be perceived as skinhead or right wing, the logo is just so damned strong, and what's more, the war's been over for fifty years."

Perhaps this is also the rationale for designers who use nazified forms as logos for skateboard and hip sportswear clients. In an age when the crucifix has been reduced to a stylish fashion accessory, images reminiscent of Nazi totalitarianism and neo-Nazi racism are exposed to an ever-younger market. In the October 1995 issue of Thrasher, a skateboard monthly that dabbles in alternative politics, advertisements for skateboards exhibit overt and covert Germanic/Nazi influences. Among them, the Iron Cross, the traditional German army medal for valor (indeed the only medal that Hitler ever wore on his tunic), appears as a component of an Old English logotype for Beer City Skateboards; a Kiss/SS-inspired lightning bolt is the centerpiece in the Germanic spiky Fraktur type for the Real Skateboard logo (Fraktur, incidentally, was one of the two official typefaces of the Third Reich); a variant of a Flemish SS divisional badge

TOP: Badge for a Flemish SS division, c. 1936.

BOTTOM: Logo for Vision Street Wear, c. 1989.

Various SS division badges, c. 1936.

is part of the logo for Vision Street Wear; and the logo for Focus skateboards draws its striking form from a combination of SS and other neo-fascist emblems. The above can be explained, though not excused, as mindless nostalgic sampling, but other applications reveal a more sinister influence.

A tear-and-peel sticker with the logo for a Los Angeles rock band, Follow For Now, is almost identical to the mark for the Aryan Nations, a neo-Nazi hate group linked to a variety of political assassinations. The sampling of this logo does not trivialize the movement of hate. Those designers who believe that they are doing the world a service by reducing the symbols of brutality to the equivalent of happy faces are deluding themselves.

Logo for Focus skateboards with swastika influence, ca. 1990.

"We see the competition for market supremacy as a big game: Battle of the Logo-Dinosaurs or Clash of the Icon Titans or something. On this level, it sounds fun and we just want to join in," claimed Ian Anderson, a member of Designers Republic, the innovative English graphic design firm that specializes in music packaging, in an interview in *Emigre* #30.

In the spirit of logo demystification, Designers Republic has commandeered and reconfigured various multinational brands in the service of their hip clients. Most are benign-enough samplings of mainstream corporate trademarks. But in a letter to the editor in Emigre #31, Jeffrey Keedy restates and critiques DR's position on the sampling of logos: "I guess I worry that since there is no hierarchy in the Age of Plunder and whatever captures the imagination in a split second is what's important, DR will appropriate the swastika because it is a cool-looking symbol and if anyone can make it look even cooler DR can."

Indeed one of their pieces, a promotional T-shirt for Supersonic, is a bitmapped derivation of the Nazi-era logo for the Deutsche Arbeitsfront (German Workers Front), the 25 million–man cadre of German workers that served as the bulwark of the Nazi regime. Granting that the Designers Republic's image distorts the original symbol of an eagle with talons holding a machine gear and eliminates the swastika originally found in that gear, it nevertheless remains a flagrant abuse of the past and, perhaps unbeknownst to DR, a variant of an emblem currently used by an outlawed neo-Nazi group in Germany.

Logo for the rock band, Follow For Now, 1992.

The Nazis arguably began the popular chic for wearing logos and emblems. Nazi icons were strong enough to seduce a nation and still contain a graphic power that can be unleashed today. This is not simply the allure of a well-designed form, like the Coca-Cola logo, nor is it the stuff of nostalgic fads, like hula hoops and "flower power" buttons. It is the embodiment of a rare and dangerous hypnotic quality that expresses the passions, emotions, and aspirations of the masses. Playing with it is playing with fire, which is why the most dangerous pyromaniac in the past couple of years is a rock band called The Residents and their album graphics for *Third Reich and Roll*.

Embedded in a visually dense package are pictures of Hitlerian characters and Nazi images (the CD disk is a

Logo for the Aryan Nations, c. 1980.

CD package and interior album graphics for Sacred Reich, c. 1993.

pattern of swastikas, and the band's logo is a six-pointed star medallion of German eagles with a swastika in the center). The package was considered contraband in Germany, where it was called Censored and Roll. But in the United States, it was just another example of "shock rock." And appearances to the contrary, "Third Reich and Roll is no neo-Nazi hate rock group album but a scathingly satirical look at sixties bubble-gum rock somehow twisted into a shocking seventies bubble-gum avant guard [*sic*]. With a swift kick in the balls . . . ," say the liner notes, that truly tests the limits of satire — and fails. This is more like R. Crumb's lamely parodic pair of comic strips published in *Weirdo* in 1994 that satirically told of how the dirty niggers and Jews would take over America. The

144

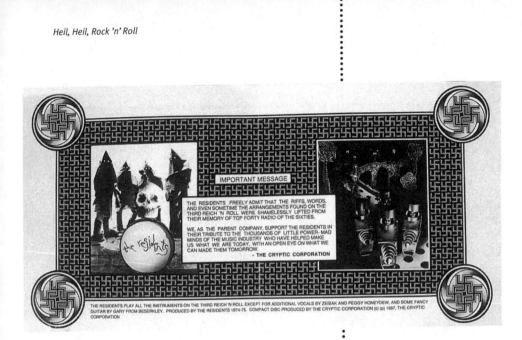

strips were reprinted last year (without permission), as if they were real hate propaganda, in *Race & Reality*, an international neo-Nazi magazine. Third Reich and Roll attempts to toe the fine line between reality and humor and falls prey to stupidity.

History reveals many brilliant examples of how Hitler and his henchmen were humorously ridiculed for propagandistic purposes during and after the rise of the Nazis in Germany. Charlie Chaplin's film, *The Great Dicta-tor*, makes the person of Hitler into a megalomaniacal clown and the swastika into "The Double Cross." And as anti-Nazi attacks go, John Heartfield reclaimed the fascists' own symbols as the basis for caustic and acerbic caricatures in AIZ, the Communist workers' magazine.

When he made the swastika from four blood-dripping executioner's axes, Heartfield was not poking fun, but revealing the truth about the regime. The imagery always hit its target, whereas a misfire like Third Reich and Roll is easily misconstrued and ultimately supports the forces of evil.

As Nazi atrocities are challenged by revisionist historians who brazenly question the conclusive evidence of mass genocide (or in today's argot, "ethnic cleansing"), the trivialization of symbols contributes to the real threat that these acts will someday be reduced to a historical footnote. Designers and artists who ignorantly play with the swastika and other Nazi emblems are not only perpetrating a crime against history, they are mutilating a universal language. The various symbols devised by the Nazi image makers are a vivid reminder of systematic torture and murder. These pictures, signs, and emblems are not merely clip art for designers. They are evidence of crimes against humanity and should remain so.

chapter seven

REDEMPTION IMPOSSIBLE

"Sometimes, to paraphrase Freud, a manji is not a manji... But sometimes, a manji—a centuries-old religious symbol of good fortune in Buddhism and Hinduism—can be mistaken for a swastika."

—"Pokémon, Minus Manji Symbol," *Newsday*, December 10, 1999

Logo for Falun Gong, 1999.

In Asia and India, the swastika has never borne the same signification that it does in the late–twentieth-century West. Today, it is still used on commercial signs and in religious ritual. In 1998, a sizable cult of Chinese Buddhists, The Falun Gong, challenged the atheistic policies of the government of the People's Republic of China, which, in 1999, first banned the group, indicted its leader-in-exile, and outlawed their emblem, a swastika. The Falun Gong version uses the counterclockwise swastika in a circle surrounded by four monad or yin-yang marks. It is neither Nazi nor anti-Semetic; it is based on the Falun or "law wheel," in reference to Buddhist law's eternal nature. According to an article in the *Wall Street*

Journal, "In China's Religious Crackdown, an Ancient Symbol Gets the Boot" (September 9, 1999), police have been stopping tourist busses with swastikas painted on the sides and have harassed monks carrying bags of incense bearing the swastika.

Given this symbolic usage, should the swastika be denied to those who consider it sacred? Some believe that it is profanation to refer to the swastika as evil, for it condemns its worshipers for crimes they did not commit. Certain advocates fervently believe that the swastika has been held hostage by the Nazis for too long and that the time has come to reclaim it—much like the words "queer" and "nigger" have been repossessed by victims of these slurs.

Reclamation of the swastika is inevitable for some, if only through art. The Friends of the Swastika, for example, is a grassroots organization founded by the artist known as Man Woman, who maintains a site on the World Wide Web that is designed to end "swastika-phobia" and displays examples of the non-Nazi iterations from the past and present (including the work of contemporary "primitive" body piercers and tattoo artists). His "vision statement" affirms that "This Web site has no connections to any racist propaganda. We do not deny the pain... of the Second World War and

ManWoman
ManWoman's art
ManWoman's book
email
friends of the swastika

Friends of the Swastika
Say to Hell with Hitler!

Swastika Declaration of Independence, April 1995

This is a manifesto by the Friends of the Swastika, some of whom met in Cranbrook, British Columbia in April 1995 and ten years earlier in Swastika, Ontario in April of 1985, to support the re-integration of the swastika as a good luck sign and sacred symbol. The founding members of the Friends of the Swastika, ManWoman, Guru Svastika, Douglas Youngblood, and Carolyn O'Neil (the town historian), held their first meeting and Swastika Conference in Swastika, Ontario in 1985. Residents of Swastika, Ontario had to fight hard to keep their town's name during the Second World War. The Canadian government wanted to change it to "Winston" to honor Churchill.

The swastika has been a symbol of benediction for more than five thousand years in almost every culture of the world, including the Jews. It has been the hope of many human beings of different belief, race and color for prosperity and brotherhood.

The swastika had universal status in a non-political way until it was misused by Adolf Hitler in the Second World War. The common view of the swastika in the West then became the opposite of the original benign, happy symbol. It became the most dreaded of all signs—tarnished with the horrors of war. Now, it is still being used by skin-heads and terrorists to intimidate law-abiding citizens. On the other hand, over half of the world's population still honors the swastika in the Hindu and Buddhist traditions.

The Friends of the Swastika is a non-political, grass-roots group of friends anyone can be a part of. It is the aim of FOTS to detoxify the swastika through education for use in its original meaning—the auspicious energy at the center of life. If enough people agree, it will change! We, the undersigned, after years of collective interest and research, declare the swastika to be innocent of the crimes perpetrated in its name under the Nazi banners. Five years of war cannot be allowed to wipe out five thousand years of sacred history. We declare that the swastika has an independent life. We say, "To hell with Hitler"!

Sign the declaration!
and read what others have had to say

Warning: there is a limit of approximately 150 words on the guestbook/declaration- stay concise!

Many people have signed it—including Lyle Tuttle, Leo Zulueta, Clayton Patterson, Charles Gatewood, Billy Shire, Spider Webb, Robert Delford Brown, Bob Roberts, Hanky Panky, Joe Coleman, Chris Pfouts, Steve Bonge, Jack Rudy, Jonathan Shaw, Paul Jeffries, Skull and Katzen—to name a few of the more famous.

HOPI

CHRISTIAN

MALTA

TIBET

CEYLON

CHINA

JAPAN

ISLAMIC

LAPLAND

HINDU

CELT

BALI

AZTEC

JAIN

GREEK

JEWISH

Web page for Friends of the Swastika, 1999.

the Holocaust. We feel that the time is ripe to put the Nazi decade into the proper context in full view of the ten thousand years of suppressed swastika history and to let the swastika get on with its benign life." Towards this end, in 1995 Man Woman issued a "Declaration of Independence" proclaiming the innocence of the swastika (signed by artists, poets, and tattooers) and created a new emblem called the "Gentle Swastika," in which the mark is nested by doves of peace. Through the Internet Man Woman has developed a core of sympathizers who believe that the symbol can be cleansed through continuous positive applications.

It is hard to believe, however, that anyone closely touched by the Holocaust or racism can view the swastika without feeling the pain it represents. Yet artist Edith Altman, a student of a Lubavitcher rabbi in Chicago, mounted an installation titled "Reclaiming the Symbol/The Art of Memory," which challenges such assumptions. As reported in the magazine *Tikkun* (Vol. 14, No. 4), Altman was motivated by the concept of tikkun olam or "repair of the world." This art piece, which she began in 1988, is devoted to restoring the swastika to its pre-Nazi meaning—the triumph of good over evil that is addressed in certain Kabbalistic texts. The work includes a gold, wall-sized pre-Nazi swastika (reading

Swastik soap package, India, 1999.

Swastika photography studio in Malaysia, 1997. Photograph by Marcia Lippman.

from right to left) and a black Nazi version on the floor (reading from left to right). Inspired by her own experience of Kristalnacht (the officially sanctioned vandalizing of Jewish businesses and synagogues throughout Nazi Germany), Altman argues that she wanted to neutralize the symbol and reinvest it with ancient meaning.

Manuel Ocampo is another painter who attacks taboos and stereotypes through art that quotes all kinds of religious and cultural symbology. Among the recurring themes, he challenges the provenance of the swastika. "I don't want to give it a literal reading because I don't mean for my work to be read didactically," he explained in an e-mail. "Formally (visually) speaking, it is a powerful icon. And I think the plural (or what many people see as dual) personalities it possesses is what makes the image a compelling one to consider." As far as the swastika being beyond redemption, Ocampo argues that it is more an issue for Europeans and White Americans. "Walking through a Chinese supermarket in Monterey Park (Los Angeles) one can find a large red swastika hanging over the refrigerated noodle section," he added. "It is obvious that there is a plurality of contexts in which the symbol is found. And of course the meaning is always found in the eyes of the beholder and how they've been trained to read signs."

On the surface the duality that Ocampo refers to is a viable excuse for reevaluating the swastika's role. And in this sense a British photographer, Gavin Fernandes, also tried to return the symbol to its ancient Indian and Chinese roots in a series of art/fashion photographs shown at a 1999 exhibition promoting Asian culture at the ooozerozerozero Gallery in London. The images, which are blown up to poster size, stylishly show Asian models both situated against and wearing swastika ornaments. The artist's intent was to present the swastika as it was in antiquity, through signs that appear

Swastika graffiti in Germany, c. 1992.

in orange, yellow, and red, avoiding black completely. The images are aesthetically keen and graphically startling, but the matter-of-fact use of the swastika is nonetheless disturbing. The artist argues that desecration of the swastika by Westerners is an insult to Asian peoples, who deserve the same consideration as those who were terrorized by it. But the idea of shocking an unwitting populace to accept the swastika in its benign form seems beyond the power of even the most well-intentioned art.

In the 1973 film *Sleeper*, Woody Allen sarcastically predicted that in the distant future, the swastika will be worn as a fashion accessory. What once seemed implausible seems perfectly sound today. Has the time come so soon? Can the swastika truly be seized from those who defiled it? Can such a criminally indicted mark, regardless of its innocent origins, be rehabilitated? Can the same image that represents the Holocaust ever represent anything else? Will those who suffered the Holocaust or live in its shadow ever see a scrawled swastika on a door or wall as a goodwill gesture?

Even as this book was going to press a controversy erupted regarding the swastika on Pokémon cards, the hot game produced by the Japanese-owned Nintendo. As reported by the Associated Press on December 3, 1999, a ten-year-old boy in Lynbrook, New York, bought a package of the Japanese version of these highly collectible cards. His parents were surprised to find that on two different cards were printed "manji," the mirror image of the Nazi swastika. After protests from the boy's parents and subsequent complaints, Nintendo of America announced that the card would be discontinued. "What is appropriate for one culture may not be of another," said a company spokesman. The Anti-Defamation league reported that the decision "showed sensitivity to the feelings of Jews and others

to whom the swastika is a very offensive symbol...
We recognize there was no intention to be offensive,
but goods flow too easily from one place to another in
the world. The notion of isolating it in Asia would just
create more problems." Meanwhile, Larry Rosenweig,
a Jew who is director of the Morikami Museum and
Japanese Gardens in Delray Beach, Florida, told the
Associated Press that opposition to the symbol was
"misplaced indignation."

On the scales of meaning the horror that the
swastika evokes far outweighs any benign attributes
it may have. For every naïve rock-and-roller who thinks
the swastika can be used with irony, there is a fervent
neo-Nazi who uses it with malice. For every well-meaning
artist who thinks the swastika can be tamed, there is
a devout racist who embraces it. That the swastika
prompts such complex debate only goes to prove that
that debate is a smoke screen. As long as it embodies
even an iota of evil, it will never again be redeemed.

THE SYMBOL
REDEEMED?

Desecrated Jewish gravestones in Germany, c. 2000.

Madrid [September 21, 2007] Spanish fashion chain Zara has withdrawn a handbag from its stores after a customer in Britain complained swastikas were embroidered on it.

—Reuters

Coronado, Calif. [September 26, 2007] The U.S. Navy has decided to spend as much as $600,000 for landscaping and architectural modifications to obscure the fact that one of its building complexes looks like a swastika from the air.

—Los Angeles Times.

The very first response I received upon publication of *The Swastika: A Symbol Beyond Redempton?* was a lengthy letter accusing me of "cultural colonialism," written by a Native American graphic designer, who was then living in the Southwest but had earlier attended the School of Visual Arts in New York. He was not so much angry as profoundly disappointed. After admitting he had been looking forward to the book, believing I would handle the issue "with sophistication and sensitivity," he voiced his shock at what he claimed was my wholesale disregard of the swastika's rightful place in the symbolic liturgy of his and other cultures in the Americas and elsewhere. By arguing against redemption and implicitly denying the existence of an untarnished swastika in the twenty-first century, I was perpetuating the same kind of cultural co-optation that has plagued Native Americans since the first trademark with a generic Indian was used to promote a commercial tobacco product back in the nineteenth century.

Frankly, he was right.

But I was *not* wrong.

Since 2000 when *The Swastika: A Symbol Beyond Redempton?* was first published, I have been asked numerous times, at lectures, seminars, classes, and by magazine and radio interviewers if I truly believe the swastika is indeed beyond redemption now and forever. Because the title of the book is written in the form of a question, the conclusion was not necessarily going to be definitive. There must be room for discussion, debate, even reevaluation on this issue, and I always welcome different viewpoints when presenting my polemic (and this is a polemical history, not a linear, narrative one) to students and the public. I remember being a guest on one radio call-in show shortly after publication, when an elderly woman from the Midwest asked me whether she should destroy a blanket with a swastika given to her when she was a little girl by her grandmother. She was clearly concerned that by retaining this artifact she was

Izzue clothing stores in Hong Kong (2003) display Nazi flags and banners as part of their decor.

doing something bad. I said she should definitely keep the gift because it was made long before the Nazis came to power, and it obviously had deep sentimental value for her. Clearly not all swastikas represent the same thing.

Understanding the complexities around the swastika is important. Nevertheless, and contrary to the book's title, I do end the first edition by strenuously questioning the symbol's ultimate redemption. And I particularly object to the misappropriation of the Nazi swastika by punk rockers and skateboard companies who I accuse of mindlessly using the symbol for affect—

Comic book version of "Hansi: The Girl Who Loved the Swastika" published by Chriatian Comics.

and, believe me, I'm being generous in using the term "mindlessness." Yet stupid applications of the swastika today—like in 2006 when a Hong Kong fashion chain, IZZUE, produced a range of T-shirts and pants with Nazi symbols printed on them—are not my only *betes noir*.

As long as Nazi icons are knowingly used as tools (and weapons) of prejudice and hate (witness the many scrawls on grave stones and synagogues around the world), then it is impossible to justify returning the swastika to its original meaning, particularly in Western societies where the history is still fresh in the mass con- sciousness—yes, even after over half a century. More- over, and this is key for me, given that each passing year there are fewer and fewer survivors of the Holocaust, the swastika must remain one of the principle mnemonics of this horrific epoch; to reprieve it would constitute a grave injustice to the victims of genocide.

My understanding as a designer and educator of how powerful signs and symbols are over mass and individual conscious and subconscious leads me to the conclusion that images that stand for evil (if only for a brief period) should not be rehabilitated without under- going considerable circumspection. And what symbol embodies more evil in this era than the swastika?

The reason for writing the book in the first place was to argue the point as much with myself as with readers. After all, much is "felt" about the swastika (pro and con) but less is truly known about it. Given its extraordinary longevity and expansive diaspora, as already explained in this book, it is imperative that we reflect on its historical convolution before passing definitive judgments. Admittedly, I had a bias going into the project, but I also honestly wanted to find ways of mitigating it, of "feeling" differently. But in the end, while I am not calling outright for a ban (what kind of liberal would I be), I embrace a position that may indeed be justifiably viewed as "cultural colonialism." Just as certain words and images are taboo in specific contexts and cultures for any number of more trivial reasons, the swastika, while not the literal perpetrator of the crime, was one of the symbolic weapons used in its execution. So, like a proponent of gun control, I am an advocate of swastika control.

I'm not alone in this view. Clearly the two events quoted at the top of this essay prove that in the West, the swastika remains charged. While the Zara handbag was made in India where the green swastika, which was woven into the corners, was done without malice as a token of luck, it was perceived as vile. Although the navy barracks built in the shape of a swastika could never be seen as such on the ground, users of Google Earth found it and voiced their objections. These are only two of many similar responses today to the ancient sign.

There are, however, vocal dissenters who fervently argue Hitler's usurpation of the swastika was merely an aberration and that the statute of limitations is now over. Others insist that only by prying the Nazi grip off the

166

swastika, reclaiming it, and restoring it to the original benign meaning, can Hitler's tyranny over it be expunged. There are still others who ask, rightly, why the Hammer and Sickle is not perceived as harshly, since under Stalin more people were imprisoned or murdered. And then there are those who simply refuse to cede the symbol to the forces of evil without a fight. I sympathize with these views, but I can also come up with counter arguments: Nazism was an aberration, but a decidedly incredible one, and the swastika came to symbolize the worst that man can do to man. Reclaiming its original meaning is fine, but that should not mean somehow ignoring its Nazi implications. The Hammer and Sickle, created after the October Revolution, stood not for Lenin or Stalin but for the Soviet Union. Stalin had no part in designing it and it stood for the nation long after his death. Conversely, the swastika was synonymous with Hitler, in large part because it was "his" symbol for "his" regime. Now, as far as evil is concerned, a combination of historical fact and Allied propaganda made the swastika an indelible sign of horror, whether we like it or not.

I'm willing to admit that my own viewpoint is plagued by emotionalism. I have been criticized for writing a "personal" history, not a dispassionate narrative. Nonetheless, reason does play a part in my firm

Swastika painted on Indian store wall, representing good fortune.

stand against redemption in Western cultures. The German government's long-term prohibition of its public display in Germany, except for historical documentary purposes (even in flea markets today, black markers or tape obliterates the image on wartime memorabilia), was legislated not because the Nazis were just one of many repressive regimes that lost a war and faded into history. It was a paradigm of how terror became the official policy of a civilized state and how a populace was seduced into accepting its crimes (in fact, how crimes were made legal, as Hitler would say, "under the swastika"). Regimes come and go either by force or election—even the defeated Italian Fascists and their face's emblem is viewed (rightly or wrongly) by history without the same revulsion as the Nazis—but only once in the twentieth century has a totalitarian entity as the Nazis with such extraordinary symbolic trappings been such a touchstone—and prime example—of the worst instincts of mankind. Politics alone does not explain why the Allies sought to stamp out all traces of Nazism in their denazification period. They understood how effectively Hitler inveigled his way into the young generation. In truth, and given its own hypocritical opportunism, because the U.S. failed to eliminate the Nazis (the State Department allowed many into the U.S.), banning the swastika was little more than a symbolic gesture, albeit one I support.

The swastika is a tragic case. It is a historical irony that this ancient manifestation of good luck and fortune bears such a horrible stigma. But from the moment it was adopted by the Nazis, it became a mark (and as I said before, a weapon) of hate. Misappropriated as it was, Hitler referred to it as an anti-Semitic emblem under which his forces would exclude the enemy from all facets of German life. Once it was introduced as the Nazi logo, there was no turning back. Obviously, many people felt that way back in the twenties and thirties, and many individuals and companies (from Rudyard Kipling to Coca Cola) who used the swastika longer than it was in Nazi hands for commercial or personal reasons rejected any connection to it. The same principle should apply today. I believe not enough time has passed before the negative connotations are shed. Which begs the big question: what is enough time?

ABOUT
THE AUTHOR

Steven Heller is the co-founder and co-chair (with Lita Talarico) of the MFA Designer As Author program and the co-founder (with Alice Twemlow) of the MFA in Design Criticism at the School of Visual Arts. For thirty-three years he was an art director at the *New York Times* and currently writes the "Visuals" column for the *New York Times Book Review*. He is the editor of *AIGA VOICE* and contributing editor to *Print*, *ID*, *Eye*, and *Baseline* magazines. He is the author, co-author, or editor of over 120 books. In 2007, he received the Masters Series Award and exhibition at the School of Visual Arts in New York.

SELECTED
BIBLIOGRAPHY

Books

Adam, Peter. *Art of the Third Reich*. New York: Harry N. Abrams, Inc. Publishers, 1992.

Bauer, Bartel. *Hakenkreuz und Mythos*. Munich: Verlag von Piloin & Loehle, 1934.

Baynes, Norman H., ed. *The Speeches of Adolf Hitler: April 1922–August 1939*. London: Oxford University Press, 1942.

Blavatsky, H. P. *The Secret Doctrine: The Synthesis of Science, Religion, and Philosophy*. Adelphi, W. C.: The Theosophical Publishing Company, Limited, 1888.

Bok, Edward. *The Americanization of Edward Bok*. New York: Charles Scribner's Sons, 1920.

Brinton, Daniel G. The Ta Ki, *The Svastika and the Cross in America*. Philadelphia: Press of MacCalla & Company, 1889.

Brown, W. Norman. *The Swastika: Study of the Nazi Claims of its Aryan Origin*. New York: Emerson Books, Inc., 1933.

Budge, Sir E. A. Wallis. *Amulets and Talismans*. New Hyde Park, New York: University Books, 1962.

Butts, Edward. *The Triskelion*. Kansas City, Missouri: Burton Publishing Company, 1921.

Carr, Joseph J. *The Twisted Cross*. Shreveport, Louisiana: Huntington House, 1985.

Cavendish, Richard. *Mythology*. New York: Rizzoli International Publication, Inc., 1930.

Cirlot, J. E. *A Dictionary of Symbols*. New York: Philosophical Library Inc., date unknown.

Cleary, William. *Surfing: All the Young Wave Hunters*. New York: Signet Books, 1967.

Crowley, Aleister. *Magick Without Tears*. Saint Paul, Minnesota: Llewellyn Publications, 1973.

Conquergood, Chas. R. *The Moral of Two German Marks*. Montreal, Canada: Montreal Club of Printing House Craftsmen, 1942.

Cunningham, Alexander. *The Stupa of Bharhut: A Buddhist Monument*. Varanasi, India: Indological Book House, 1962.

Davis, Renée. *La Croix Gammée Cette Énigme*. Paris: Presses De La Cité, date unknown.

Dreyfuss, Henry. *Symbol Sourcebook: An Authorative Guide to International Graphic Symbols*. New York: McGraw Hill, 1972.

The Encyclopaedia Britannica (Eleventh Edition) Vol VII. New York: The University Press, 1910.

Fisch, Rabbi Dr. S., ed. *Ezekiel*. London: The Soncino Press, date unknown.

Fischer, Klaus P. *Nazi Germany: A New History*. New York: Continuum, 1995.

Flowers, Stephen E., ed. *The Secret of the Runes by Guido Von List*. Rochester, Vermont: Destiny Books, 1988.

Goldsmith, Elizabeth E. *Life Symbols as Related to Sex Symbolism*. New York: G. P. Putnam's Sons, 1924.

Goodrick-Clark, Nicholas. *The Occult Roots of Nazism: Secret Aryan Cults and Their Influence on Nazi Ideology*. New York: New York University Press, 1985.

Goodrick-Clark, Nicholas. *Hitler's Priestess: Savitri Devi, the Hindu-Aryan Myth, and Neo-Nazism*. New York: New York University Press, 1998.

Hayes, Will. *The Swastika: A Study in Comparative Religion*. Chatham, England: the Order of the Great Companion, 1934.

Hebdige, Dick. *Subculture: The Meaning of Style*. London: Routledge, 1979.

Hitler, Adolf. *Mein Kampf*. New York: Reynal & Hitchcock, 1941.

Hoffmann, Paul. *The Viennese: Spendor, Twilight, and Exile*. New York: Anchor Press, Doubleday, 1988.

Humbert, Claude. *Ornamental Design*. New York: Viking Press, 1970.

The Jewish Encyclopedia. New York: Funk and Wagnalls Company, 1901.

Koch, Rudolf. *The Book of Signs*. London: The First Editions Club, 1930.

Lechler, Jörg. *Dom Hakenkreuz*. Leipzig, Germany: Verlag von Curt Kabizsch, 1921.

Mackenzie, Kenneth R.H., ed. *The Royal Masonic Cyclopaedia*. Northhampton-shire, England: The Aquarian Press, 1987.

Mosse, L. George. *The Facist Revolution: Toward a General Theory of Fascism*. New York: Howard Fertig, 1999.

Nazi Kitsch. Darmstadt, Germany: Verlag KG, 1975.

Nuttall, Zelia. *Archaeological and Ethnological Papers of the Peabody Museum Harvard University* Vol II. Cambridge, Massachusetts: Museum Publications, 1901.

Occupation of Germany: Policy and Progress, 1945–46. Washington, D.C.: United States Government Printing Office. The Department of State, United States of America, Publications 2783.

Peterson, Edward N. *The Limits of Hitler's Power*. Princeton, New Jersey: Princeton University Press, 1969.

Pia, Jack. *Nazi Regalia*. New York: Ballantine Books Inc., 1971.

Prange, Gordon W. *Hitler's Words*. Washington, D.C.: American Council on Public Affairs, 1946.

Price, Billy F. *Adolf Hitler: The Unknown Artist*. Houston, Texas: Billy F. Price Publishing Co., 1984.

Proctor, Robert N. *The Nazi War on Cancer*. Princeton, New Jersey: Princeton University Press, 1999.

Quinn, Malcom. *The Swastika: Constructing The Symbol*. London and New York: Routledge, 1997.

Sanders, Ed. *The Family: The Story of Charles Manson's Dune Buggy Attack Battalion*. New York: E. P. Dutton and Co. Inc., 1971.

Schliemann, Dr. Henry. Tiryns: *The Prehistorical Palace of the Kings of Tiryns*. New York: Charles Scribner's Sons, 1885.

Schuman, Frederick L. *The Nazi Dictatorship: A Study in Social Pathology and the Politics of Fascism*. New York: Alfred A. Knopf, 1936.

Shanks, Hershel. *Judaism in Stone: The Archaeology of Ancient Synagogues*. New York: Harper & Row Publishers, 1979.

Sklar, Dusty. *The Nazis and the Occult*. New York: Dorset Press, 1977/1989.

Smith, Whitney. *Flags Thoughout the Ages and Across the World*. New York: McGraw-Hill Book Company, 1976.

Wilhelm II, Kaiser. *Die Chinesische Monade*. Liepzig, Germany: Verlag von K. F. Koehler, 1934.

Wilson, Thomas. *The Swastika: The Earliest Known Symbol, and its Migrations; With Observations on the Migration of Certain Industries in Prehistoric Times*. Washington, D.C.: The Smithsonian Institute, U.S. National Museum, 1896.

Wise, James Waterman. *Swastika: The Nazi Terror*. New York: Harrison Smith and Robert Haas, 1933.

Wistrich, Robert S. *Weekend in Munich: Art Propaganda and Terror in the Third Reich*. London: Pavilion Books Ltd., 1995.

Articles

Astley, Dr. H. J. D. "The Swastika: A Study." *The Quest*, January 1925.

Baigell, Matthew. "Kabbalah and Jewish-American Artists." *Tikkun*, Vol. 14, No. 4.

Blanchard, Tamsin. "Here Comes the Sun." *The Observer Magazine*, July 11, 1999.

Feeney, Corinne B. "Arch-Isolationists, the San Blas Indians." *National Geographic*, February 1941.

Levy, Andrew. "The Swastikas of Niketown." *Harpers Magazine*, April 1996.

Lois, George. "The Five Greatest Logos." *Adweek*, January 18, 1982.

Smith, Craig S. "Influential Devotees at Core of Chinese Movement." *Wall Street Journal*, April 27, 1999.

Stermer, Dugald. "The Father of Advertising." *Ramparts*, April 1967.

Tolischus, Otto D. "The Reich Adopts Swastika As Nation's Official Flag; Hitler's Replay to 'Insult.'" *The New York Times*, September 16, 1935.

INDEX

Books from Allworth Press

Teaching Motion Design: Course Offerings and Class Projects from the Leading Undergraduate and Graduate Programs
edited by Steven Heller and Michael Dooley (paperback, 6 x 9, 288 pages, $21.95)

Teaching Graphic Design
edited by Steven Heller (paperback, 6 x 9, 288 pages, $19.95)

How to Think Like a Great Graphic Designer
by Debbie Millman (paperback, 6 x 9, 256 pages, $24.95)

Green Graphic Design
by Brian Doherty with Celery Design Collaborative (paperback, 6 x 9, 208 pages, $24.95)

Looking Closer 5: Critical Writings on Graphic Design
edited by M. Bierut, W. Drenttel, and S. Heller (paperback, $6\frac{3}{4}$ x $9\frac{1}{2}$, 302 pages, $21.95)

Looking Closer 4: Critical Writings on Graphic Design
edited by M. Bierut, W. Drenttel, and S. Heller (paperback, $6\frac{3}{4}$ x $9\frac{1}{2}$, 304 pages, $21.95)

Advertising Design and Typography
by Alex White (paperback, $8\frac{3}{4}$ x $11\frac{1}{4}$, 224 pages, $50.00)

Design Literacy: Understanding Graphic Design, Second Edition
by Steven Heller and Karen Pomeroy (paperback, $6\frac{3}{4}$ x 10, 288 pages, $19.95)

Looking Closer 3: Classic Writings on Graphic Design
edited by Michael Bierut, Jessica Helfand, Steven Heller, and Rick Poynor (paperback, $6\frac{3}{4}$ x 10, 304 pages, $18.95)

AIGA Professional Practices in Graphic Design, Second Edition
The American Institute of Graphic Arts, edited by Tad Crawford (paperback, 6 x 9, 320 pages, $29.95)

Business and Legal Forms for Graphic Designers
by Tad Crawford and Eva Doman Bruck (softcover, $8\frac{1}{2}$ x 11, 240 pages, includes CD-ROM, $24.95)

Please write to request our free catalog or to order by credit card, call 1-800-491-2808.

To see our complete catalog on the World Wide Web, or to order online, you can find us at *www.allworth.com*.